# THE BEAUTY OF JERUSALEM
# JERUSALEM
## AND THE HOLY PLACES OF
# THE GOSPELS

G.S.P. FREEMAN-GRENVILLE

SECOND EDITION

CONTINUUM · NEW YORK

1987
The Continuum Publishing Company
370 Lexington Avenue, New York, N.Y. 10017

Copyright © 1983 by G.S.P. Freeman-Grenville
Copyright © Second Edition, revised
Maps, Diagrams, and Plans Copyright © 1983 by P. Giggle
Originally published by East-West Publications, London

All rights reserved. No part of this book may be reproduced, stored in a
retrieval system, or transmitted, in any form or by any means, electronic,
mechanical, photocopying, recording, or otherwise, without the written
permission of The Continuum Publishing Company.

Printed in Great Britain

**Library of Congress Cataloging-in-Publication Data**
Freeman-Grenville, G.S.P. (Greville Stewart Parker)
    The beauty of Jerusalem and the holy places of the Gospels.

    Reprint. Originally published: London: East-West Publications,
c1983.
    Bibliography: p.
    Includes index.
    1. Jerusalem—Description—Guide-books.   2. Christian shrines—
Jerusalem.   3. Bible. N.T. Gospels—Geography.
I. Title.   DS109.F74   1987      915.694'40454      87-5918
ISBN 0-8264-0398-0

IN FOND MEMORY OF MY
FATIIER


*Thine eyes shall see the king in his beauty.*
Isaiah 33.17

# CONTENTS

# LIST OF ILLUSTRATIONS

*Front Cover* – The Old City from the Mount of Olives

*Back Cover* – The Western ("Wailing") Wall

## LIST OF MAPS AND PLANS

## PREFACE TO THE SECOND EDITION

Knowledge of the antiquities of the Holy Land increases year by year. This edition has been amended to include discoveries between 1981 and 1986, when again my wife and I visited it. I am obliged to Fr. José Montalverne de Lancastre, OFM, to Dr Dan Bahat, and to Mr Isam Awadh, for various kindnesses.

Sheriff Hutton, York.                                 G.S.P.F.-G.
*9 February 1987*

# PREFACE TO FIRST EDITION

This is a brief historical guide to Jerusalem and the principal Holy Places of the Gospels. The evangelists had no intention of writing works of topography or history; their object was to present the teaching of Jesus Christ and the story of Redemption. It is nevertheless possible to arrange the events of his life in a reasonable, but arbitrary, order in their topographical setting. After a brief summary of the history of the Holy Land, the six itineraries start with Bethlehem, and lead up to the final drama of the Passion, Resurrection and Ascension, describing the sites and buildings associated with them. Accounts of some other relevant sites, buildings and museums have been added. Conveniently for our purpose, Israeli law defines antiquity as before AD 1700. Except for recent constructions, repairs, or archaeological exploration, this guide is not concerned with modern times.

The writer visited the Holy Places for the first time thirty-seven years ago. Since then great changes have taken place. Much of the old tawdriness has been stripped away. There have been remarkable and illuminating archaeological discoveries. Many authenticate long hallowed traditions. In the *Haram al-Sharif* (The Noble Sanctuary), the Dome of the Rock, the Mosque of al-Aqsa, and likewise in the Basilica of the Holy Sepulchre, expert restorations have taken place or still proceed. For the most part we see these and other buildings in a state far better than for many centuries. Especially noteworthy is the restoration by the Israeli Antiquities Service of part of the Herodian pavement in the Via Dolorosa, on which Jesus may have trodden to carry his Cross. We who are privileged to tread where he trod are all in the debt of those who have made it possible.

There are very many to whom my thanks are due for many kindnesses while this guide has been in preparation. Especially must I mention the Most Reverend Father Custos of the Holy Land, OFM, Bishop Guregh Kapikian, Mr George Hintlian, Fr. José Montalverne de Lancastre, OFM, Bro. Fabian Adkins, OFM, Mr Isam Awadh, and also members of the British School of Archaeology in Jerusalem. I am likewise grateful to the Archdeacon of York, the Venerable Leslie Stanbridge, who took the typescript with him on the recent pilgrimage he led to the Holy Land. There are others yet too numerous to name. They all have my deepest gratitude.

Sheriff Hutton, York.                    G.S.P.F.-G.
*3 May 1983*

# INTRODUCTION

## GENERAL NOTES FOR THE VISITOR

Generally speaking, churches are open all the hours of daylight, although some open before dawn, and a few close for an afternoon siesta. The Holy Sepulchre opens daily at 4 a.m. The *Haram al-Sharif* is open from 8 a.m. until 5 p.m. It, and the mosques used for public prayers, should be avoided between 11.30 a.m. and 12.30 p.m. and between 2.45 p.m. and 3.30 p.m. All Muslim buildings are closed to non-Muslims on Fridays. Synagogues are not open to visitors after 2 p.m. on Fridays, or on Saturdays and Jewish holy days. Museums and ancient sites under the Department of Antiquities and Museums are shut on Saturdays and Jewish holy days.

Entry to churches is free, but it is customary to make a donation. In many cases free-will offerings are the principal support of the church and clergy, and the main source from which to keep buildings in repair. The Dome of the Rock, the Aqsa Mosque and other public monuments and museums in the care of the Department of Antiquities charge visitors for entry. Tickets are always given as receipts, and any attempt to obtain money for entry to a building or site without a ticket being offered should be firmly discountenanced. Any charges mentioned in this guide were correct at the time of going to press.

Dress should be fairly conservative; men in shorts and women in trousers or sleeveless dresses or blouses are not admitted to the Holy Sepulchre. In the Jewish quarter of Mea Shearim public notices request men and women to wear head coverings and conservative dress. It is always sensible, as well as acceptable, to wear a cardigan, for the buildings can be chilly even in summer. In a few churches the doorkeepers keep overdresses for women who are not acceptably dressed, but their provision cannot be relied upon. In mosques used for prayer both men and women must remove their shoes before entering. The reason is *not* religious, but simply to keep the mats or carpets clean. In any building in the possession of Muslims it is regarded as offensive for any non-Muslim to display any overt sign of prayer, and it can be dangerous to do so.

Within most of the Old City wheeled transport is forbidden. Visitors must watch out for small carts and for laden donkeys; it is easy to get hurt. Many streets are sandy and gritty underfoot, ruinous to leather, and unsuitable for sandals or high heels. Rubber or strong composition soles with suède or turned calf uppers are advisable. There are great variations in temperature. There can be a forty degree Fahrenheit difference in the middle of the day between Jerusalem and Jericho. In winter and spring it can be wet and windy, but snow is rare, and never lies.

Outside the Old City there are frequent and very cheap bus services, both to other parts of Jerusalem and to the rest of the country. Information about these is easily obtained from hotels and hospices, and from the Christian Information Centre near the Jaffa Gate. There are numerous taxis, but the drivers rarely use their meters. It is prudent, and essential on a long journey, to agree on the fare beforehand if the driver says he is not going to use the meter, and it is wise to make the arrangement through an hotel or other agency before a witness. Persons visiting desert areas should always carry drinking water. Those without desert experience should under no circumstance go without at least one experienced companion. On any such occasions the hotel, or some other reliable person, should always be told where one is going and the expected time of return.

Antiquities are defined by law as any object made before AD 1700. It is forbidden to take them out of Israel without a written export permit. These can be obtained from the Department of Antiquities and Museums, Rockefeller Museum, Jerusalem, tel.(02).285.151 on production of a receipt. The fee is ten percent of the purchase price. Numerous fakes are to be seen in the shops, and it is imprudent to buy antiquities or, for that matter, carpets, without independent expert advice.

Survey of Israel maps are available at most bookshops. *Jerusalem 1:14000* covers the whole urban area, and *Jerusalem: The Old City 1:2500* shows almost every street and lane. Carta Ltd, P.O.Box 2500, Jerusalem, publishes an admirable series of maps, both of the city and of the Holy Land, available in bookshops and hotel bookstalls. The Egged Bus Company publishes a map, available at its offices and bookshops, of the bus routes superimposed on the street plan.

## PLAN OF VISIT

Itineraries I to VI follow in rough outline an arbitrary chronological arrangement of the Gospels. Itinerary VI is divided into sub-sections. Itineraries I and III can, with advantage, be taken together, thus enabling II, IV and V to be followed consecutively in a single car or bus journey. It is possible, although exhausting, to complete II, IV and V in a single day. Preferably, I should take half a day; III a full day; and II, IV and V be spread over two days.

Itineraries II and V follow alternative routes between Jerusalem and Nazareth. In no circumstance should Itinerary V be attempted if there is any question of the security situation on the West Bank being doubtful. It can be perilous.

It is of course possible to spend a life time in Jerusalem, and not to have seen everything. Itinerary VI has been subdivided into six sections, covered quite easily in three days. The remaining sites listed in Itinerary VII can be visited quite easily in a single day, but it is worth leaving some extra time free to visit the museums, especially the Rockefeller Museum, surely one of the most beautiful museums in existence.

One is often asked: what can I do in a few hours, or in a day? Enter the Old City at the Damascus Gate, and pass quickly to the Via Dolorosa, and then to the Church of the Holy Sepulchre. Then proceed to the Haram al-Sharif (the Noble Sanctuary of the Dome of the Rock): visit the Dome of the Rock and the Aqsa Mosque; then walk across the courtyard to the far side, from which Gethsemane and the Mount of Olives can both be seen clearly. Then come out of the Old City at the Jaffa Gate, past the Citadel, where there are almost always taxis waiting.

## HISTORICAL INTRODUCTION

The Palestine of the Bible comprised the present state of Israel and all the remainder of the former United Nations Trust Territory of Palestine, administered as occupied territory by Israel since 1967, together with the present Kingdom of Jordan and a small part of the present Syria. The area is a narrow bridge of fertile land between the land masses of Africa and Asia, closed in on the east by desert and on the west by the Mediterranean. It has thus been the scene of constant human migrations and conquests. Only the briefest outline of its long and complex history is possible here.

## Stone Age – 800,000 BC to 4,000 BC

The earliest remains of man in Galilee have been dated to c.600,000 BC. The people were hunters and gatherers until c.14,000 BC, when men, hitherto nomadic, began to plant grain and domesticate animals. At the same time permanent villages sprang up, and pottery replaced stone vessels.

## Copper and Bronze Ages – 4,000 BC to 1,200 BC

C.4,000 BC copper was introduced, and increased trade led to the development of small towns, which were fortified. Shortly tin was alloyed with copper to produce a harder metal, bronze, and the potter's wheel replaced hand-moulded pottery. Although from time to time Egypt controlled the coastal plain, Palestine was a land of small city-states during this period. C.1800 a group of nomadic herdsmen, 318 fighting men with their families, migrated under Abraham from Ur in Chaldaea (in the present Iraq) to Hebron. C.1500 their descendants migrated to Egypt because of a famine; and c.1250 their descendants in turn migrated back, probably in two streams. Of these, one seems to have gone along the coast, while the other followed a circuitous route through the Sinai desert. About the same time the People of the Sea, whom the Bible calls Philistines, occupied coastal Palestine, incidentally providing it with a name.

## The Iron Age – 1,200 BC to 586 BC

The returning Israelites were very loosely organized under tribal leaders. Their 'judges', from whom war leaders emerged, had primarily been settlers of tribal disputes. The Philistines and the native Canaanites had a cultural superiority in their knowledge of the use of iron and of chariots. Thus the Israelites were forced to unite under a king, Saul (c.1020 BC – 1000 BC), and to learn the art of war from their enemies. The second king, David (c.1000 BC – 961 BC), consolidated the new system, conquering the stronghold of Jerusalem from the small tribe of the Jebusites. He made it the religious as well as the civil capital by bringing there the Ark of the Covenant containing the stone Tables of the Ten Commandments. In this way political unity received the sanction of religion. Under his son, Solomon (961 BC – c.922 BC), trade with neighbouring countries greatly developed. The visit of the Queen of Sheba, correctly Saba in South Arabia, which controlled the incense routes and the trading ports on the Indian Ocean, and his marriage with Pharaoh's daughter indicate his success and prestige as a monarch. However, heavy taxation and over-strict control caused the kingdom to break apart on his death. From then on there were two Israelite kingdoms: Israel, the northern one, with its capital at Samaria; and Judah, in the south, with Jerusalem as capital. In both kingdoms prophets arose, crying out against injustice and demanding purity of religion as the guarantee of political good faith. As with other monarchies, the history of the kings of Israel and Judah is marked by crimes of ambition and jealousy, and equally adorned by men of eminent virtue and prudence. The moral teaching of the prophets taught standards unique in the world of the time.

In 721 BC Israel fell to the rising power of Assyria. 27,000 of its citizens were deported. In spite of the prophet Isaiah's warning that it was political suicide, King Hezekiah of Judah allied with Egypt against Assyria, but when Sennacherib of Assyria attacked Judah c.688 BC, his army was crippled by plague, giving Hezekiah a lucky escape. His son Manasseh was forced to make peace, but Judah virtually lost its independence, regaining it only c.629/8 BC. At the end of the seventh century Judah became the vassal of Egypt. Shortly, the rising power of Babylon under Nebuchadrezzar overcame Egypt (605 BC), and Jerusalem paid tribute in 604. Then, in c.597, after a siege, Jerusalem surrendered to Babylon. Some 3,000 citizens were deported. The Jews, however, were not so easily put down. They revolted c.595/4, and again in 589, when Nebuchadrezzar began a siege that lasted eighteen months. The city fell in June 587, and was sacked. Solomon's Temple was destroyed, and more citizens deported. Yet more followed them in 582.

1. The Kedron Valley, showing Pillar of Absalom

## *Under Persia – 538 BC to 332 BC*

In a reign of nearly a generation (559-530 BC), Cyrus II the Great of Persia conquered almost all the Middle East from the eastern borders of Afghanistan to Asia Minor, and south from Syria to Egypt. So vast, so ramshackle an empire could only be held together by a tolerant and moderate government. This enabled the Jews to return from exile, and to rebuild Jerusalem (see below, p.65). If exile destroyed the Jewish polities, it had strengthened Jewish unity in religion. The rebuilt Temple now provided a single focus for religion and sacrifice, and domestic and synagogue rituals now begin to emerge as systems separate from the Temple ritual. The Persian administration used Aramaic as its official language, and it is from now on that Biblical Hebrew disappears as a spoken language.

## *Under Alexander the Great and his successors – 332 BC to 63 BC*

Alexander's career of world conquest began on the R. Danube in 335 BC, and ended at Susa in Persia in June 323. At that moment he controlled a vast area from eastern Europe to India, and Egypt and Libya. His early death and the fact that his only son was an imbecile led to the break-up of his empire among his generals. Ptolemy, the commander in Egypt, seized it and Syria. He lost Syria to the Seleucids in 315, except for Palestine. His successors held Palestine until 200 BC, when the Seleucid Antiochus III took it. Centralization of worship in the Temple of Jerusalem and foreign political control gave the Jewish High Priest a new importance. Primarily a religious figure, he now emerged as a political one. The Seleucid Antiochus IV Epiphanes initiated a policy of Hellenization in Palestine, and in 169 BC the Temple was plundered. Two years later the city was sacked. The actual cause of the war was the nomination of a High Priest who was not of the traditional Zadokite family. It led to a revolt headed by the three Maccabee brothers. In 164 they regained Jerusalem; and in 161 they made a treaty with Rome. Their Hasmonaean dynasty controlled all Palestine, the Golan, or Gaulonitis, in Syria, and much of the present Jordan, almost the area of the Kingdom of David and Solomon.

## Under Rome and Byzantium – 63 BC to AD 640

The Hasmonaean kingdom broke up in the first century BC. In 90 BC the Pharisees rebelled against Alexander Jannaeus: in the same year he was defeated by Obidath, Arab King of Nabataea on the east side of Lake Tiberias. Obidath's successor, al-Harith (Aretas) III, repeatedly defeated the Judaean army, and besieged Jerusalem. In 64, because of the unrest throughout the Middle East, Pompey came to restore order. He besieged Jerusalem in 63, and took it after three months' siege. A general settlement followed, but in 57-55 there was a further Jewish revolt. The Romans preferred indirect to direct rule. Tools lay ready to hand in the Idumaean family of Herod the Great. His sons ruled until AD 6 almost as independent rulers. Because of their incapacity, final authority was then given to a Procurator, who lived at Caesarea. Pontius Pilate held this office from 26 to 37, with the Herods under him. The ministry of Jesus took place during this period, but, from a Roman point of view, it was one incident among many of Jewish unrest. A general rebellion broke out in 40, when Caligula ordered his statue to be erected in Jerusalem. Matters were made worse by the corrupt and repressive rule of Claudius Felix, governor from 52 to 61. The finale came in 66, when the Gentiles of Caesarea massacred the Jews. The Zealots rose in Jerusalem, and murdered the Roman garrison. The Romans besieged Jerusalem, and then abandoned it. The rebellion spread throughout Judaea, Galilee and Transjordania. In 67, the Emperor Nero sent T. Flavius Vespasianus, with his son Titus, with 60,000 men and Arab auxiliaries, to put it down. Vespasian, who was proclaimed Emperor in 69, was to recover Transjordania and to encircle Judaea. In 70, after six months' siege, Titus took Jerusalem. The survivors were sold into slavery. The Sanhedrin was abolished and the Temple utterly destroyed. Its rebuilding was forbidden. Hence-forward Jews were forbidden to proselytize and subjected to a special poll tax. It was at this period that Jewish colonies spread to Arabia. Sacrificial worship had now ceased in the Temple to which it had long been confined: the priest now ceded to the Rabbi the leadership of a community that was bound together only by obedience to the Torah. In 73 Massada, the last Jewish stronghold, fell, its defenders all having committed suicide rather than surrender.

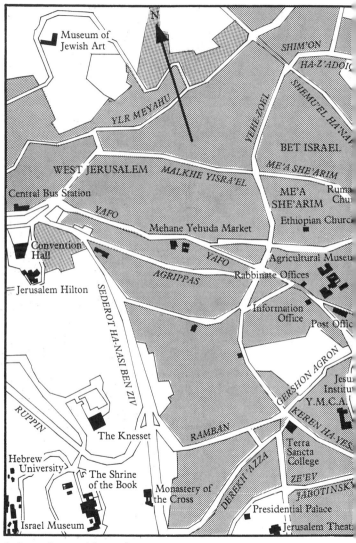

Museum of
Jewish Art

*SHIM'ON*

*HA-Z'ADOK*

*YLR MEYAHU*

*YEHE ZOEL*

*SHEMU'EL HA-NAI*

**BET ISRAEL**

WEST JERUSALEM

*MALKHE YISRA'EL*

*ME'A SHE'ARIM*

Central Bus Station

**ME'A
SHE'ARIM**

Ruma
Chu

*YAFO*

Ethiopian Church

Mehane Yehuda Market

Convention
Hall

*YAFO*

Agricultural Museum

*AGRIPPAS*

Rabbinate Offices

Jerusalem Hilton

*SEDEROT HA-NASI BEN ZIV*

Information
Office

Post Offic

*GERSHON AGRON*

Jesu
Institu

*RUPPIN*

Y.M.C.A.

*KEREN HA-YES*

*RAMBAN*

The Knesset

Terra
Sancta
College

Hebrew
University

The Shrine
of the Book

*DEREKH 'AZZA*

*ZE'EV*

*JABOTINSK*

Monastery of
the Cross

Presidential Palace

Israel Museum

Jerusalem Theat

1. Jerusalem and its environs

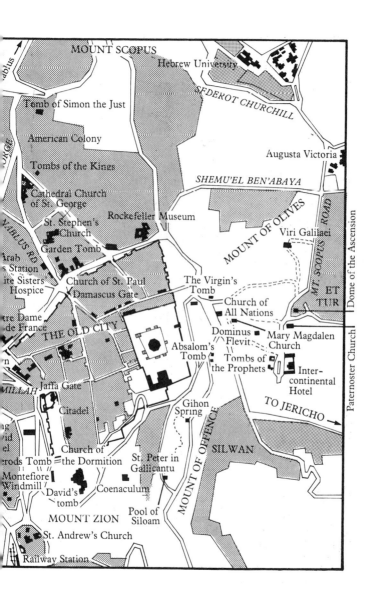

MOUNT SCOPUS

Hebrew University

SEDEROT CHURCHILL

Tomb of Simon the Just

American Colony

Augusta Victoria

Tombs of the Kings

SHEMU'EL BEN'ABAYA

Cathedral Church
of St. George

Rockefeller Museum

MOUNT OF OLIVES

Viri Galilaei

St. Stephen's
Church

Garden Tomb

NABLUS RD

Arab
s Station

ite Sisters'
Hospice

Church of St. Paul
Damascus Gate

The Virgin's
Tomb

ET
TUR

tre Dame
de France

THE OLD CITY

Church of
All Nations

Dominus
Flevit

Mary Magdalen
Church

Absalom's
Tomb

Tombs of
the Prophets

Inter-
continental
Hotel

Jaffa Gate

Citadel

Gihon
Spring

TO JERICHO

Paternoster Church

Dome of the Ascension

MT SCOPUS ROAD

Church of
erods Tomb the Dormition

St. Peter in
Gallicantu

SILWAN

Montefiore
Windmill

David's
tomb

Coenaculum

MOUNT OF OFFENCE

Pool of
Siloam

MOUNT ZION

St. Andrew's Church

Railway Station

Jewish nationalism was not extinguished. A second revolt in 132-5 was the result of the Emperor Hadrian's foundation at Jerusalem of the colony of Aelia Capitolina, with the statue of Jupiter Capitolinus on the Temple site. Between 132 and 134 fifty fortresses were razed and 455 villages destroyed, and 585,000 Jews killed. The survivors were permitted to visit Jerusalem once only in each year. Undaunted, they continued in Galilee.

The move of the imperial capital from Rome to Constantinople had no particular significance for Palestine. The Emperor Constantine's decision in 313 to make Christianity a licit religion was of permanent consequence. In 327 the Empress Helena 'discovered' the Holy Places in Jerusalem and Bethlehem, sites long known to local Christians and authenticated by Hadrian's pagan shrines. Jerusalem now became the focal point for the Christian world. Great basilicas were constructed at imperial expense, and pilgrims flocked to the Holy Land. Monasteries sprang up everywhere, and soon theological contention replaced secular violence. Before the Persian invasion of 614-29, when Chosroes (Khusrau) II seized the Cross and carried it off to Ctesiphon, the only incident of violence was the Samaritan revolt of 529.

## Under the Arabs and Tulunids – AD 640 to 969

When the Arabs defeated the Byzantines in the Yarmuk valley in 636, all Palestine and Syria fell into Muslim hands. Two years later Jerusalem itself fell to them, and the Caliph Omar came to visit the city, which was sacred to Muslims because of its connections with Abraham and the prophets, and because it was from here that the Prophet Muhammad was believed to have ascended on his mystical night-journey to heaven. Omar respected the Christian Holy Places, only building a mosque that has long since disappeared, perhaps on the site of el-Aqsa. It was not until the end of the century that, because there was a rival Caliph at Mecca, the Caliph Abd al-Malik b. Marwan decided to replace the pilgrimage to Mecca with one to Jerusalem. The *Sakhra*, or Rock, that forms the summit of Mount Moriah, on which Solomon's Temple had been built, 'shall be unto you in the place of the Kaaba.' This was the origin of the Dome of the Rock (often wrongly called the Mosque of Omar) – if not the most beautiful, certainly amongst the greatest buildings constructed by man (see p. 71-8).

After being subject to Arab governors, Palestine, with the province of Syria, fell under the Tulunid dynasty in Egypt from 870 to 905, and then again under Arab governors until 969. It remained a centre of Muslim pilgrimage, third only to Mecca and Medina.

## Under the Fatimids – 969 to 1099

In 969 the Fatimid dynasty, that had originated in Morocco, and carved out an empire from the Atlantic to the Nile, took Egypt, and Syria with it. In 1009 the Fatimid Caliph al-Hakim (1008-14) began a persecution of Christians and Jews, and soon also of his fellow-Muslims. The Church of the Holy Sepulchre was destroyed. In 1070 the Seljuq Turks under Atzig took Jerusalem. Their action in halting the now long established custom of pilgrimage to the Holy Places led to the Crusades, preached for the first time by Pope Urban II at the Council of Clermont. He had unleashed all the pent-up energy and enthusiasm of Europe. Although in 1099 the Fatimids recovered Jerusalem from the Seljuqs, nothing could stop the Crusaders. On 15 July 1099 the city fell to Geoffrey de Bouillon, and he was installed as 'baron and defender of the Holy Sepulchre', where his remains still rest.

## Under the Crusaders – 1099 to 1291

The first act of the Crusaders was to massacre all the Muslim inhabitants; by this act of monstrous cruelty they drove a wedge of hatred between Islam and Christianity. Crusader administration was efficient, and the country prospered under feudal rule. This did nothing to allay Muslim enmity, and a reconquest slowly began. The turning point was the destruction of the Crusader army by Saladin (Salah al-Din bin Ayyub) at the Horns of Hattin in Galilee on 3-4 July 1187, when Guy de Lusignan, King of Jerusalem, was taken prisoner. Jerusalem surrendered on 2 October. A century of fighting followed. In 1250 Saladin's dynasty gave way to the Bahri Mamluks. Much of Syria was taken by the Mongol Hulagu Khan in 1260, but on 3 September the Mamluks under Baybars (Sultan of Egypt 1260-77) defeated the Mongol generals decisively at Ain Jalut. The last Crusader stronghold held out at Acre (now Akko) until 1291.

## *Under the Mamluks and Ottoman Turks – 1299 to 1918*

Under the Mamluk Sultans of Egypt, Syria was a frequent battle-ground. Jerusalem, off the main route of the armies, became a back-water. It continued to attract Christian pilgrims, and there are numerous European accounts. As an intellectual centre Cairo was now paramount, and even after the Ottoman Turkish conquest of Syria (1516) and of Egypt (1517), it remained the Athens of the Muslim world. The pashas sent to govern the Ottoman provinces were political bloodsuckers, capricious and self-seeking. The land was sunk in apathy and decline. Towards the end of this period refugees from persecutions in Europe began to seek refuge in Palestine, principally Jews, but also Christians from Russia.

## *Modern Times – 1918 to the present*

The British, under General Allenby, received the surrender of Jerusa-lem on 9 December 1917. Following the Treaty of Versailles, Britain was given a League of Nations Mandate to prepare the country for eventual political independence. The persecution of Jews in Germany under Hitler, spread steadily by him throughout almost all continental Europe, led to increased immigration of Jews, who, on 2 November 1917, had been promised a 'national home' in Palestine by Lord Balfour. By 1947 continued strife between Arab and Jew led the British Labour Government to conclude that it was no longer capable of governing, and it ordered a withdrawal on 14 May 1948, when the State of Israel was proclaimed. An armistice between Israel and the neighbouring Arab powers was signed on 18 July 1948, but in 1967 war broke out again. On this occasion Israel was able to take possession of the West Bank of the River Jordan, which she still occupies, adminis-tering it under Jordanian law pending a settlement. The chequered history of the region, and its ups and downs, make any prediction of future peace imprudent.

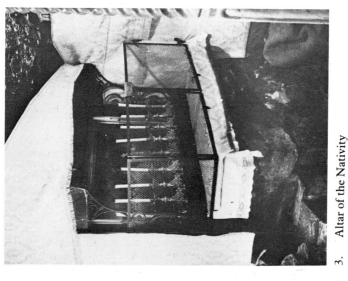

3. Altar of the Nativity

2. The Church of the Nativity, Bethlehem

## *Jerusalem to Bethlehem*

There are frequent bus services from near the Damascus and Jaffa Gates, as well as from the main bus station. Taxis are also available, and are needed for other than guided coach tours to Herodion (below, p.30).

Leaving the Jaffa Gate and crossing the Hinnom Valley to the top of the next hill, a road on the left leads to the Mount of Evil Counsel, where a site is known traditionally as Caiaphas's country house. A tree is shown with all its branches pointing eastwards: Judas Iscariot is said to have hanged himself on it. Tradition has changed its position several times.

After 3 miles (4·8 km.) on the left is the Greek Orthodox Monastery of Mar Elias, called after a bishop of that name. The tradition that connects it with Elijah (Elias), that he fled here from the wrath of Jezebel, lacks historical foundation.

At 4½ miles (7·2 km.) on the right is a small building containing the tomb of Rachel. (She has another at Rama.) It is venerated especially by Jews, but sacred also to Muslims and Christians. In appearance it is a medieval Muslim tomb. After this the road bears left at a 'Y' fork, and skirts Bethlehem on the east side. The area known as the Shepherds' Field is clearly visible in the valley below, and so too is Herod's palace stronghold of Herodion in the far distance, resembling an extinct volcano in appearance.

The Manger Square (5 miles, 8 km.) is entered from the south-east side. On the left is the courtyard of the Church of the Nativity; on the right a car park. Bethlehem is occupied almost exclusively by Christian Arabs, and since 1967 has been swollen by Arab refugees. It has been occupied continuously since the Iron Age. The Tell el-Amarna Tablets (14th c. BC) call it Bit-ilu-Lakhama, the House (or Shrine) of the goddess Lakhama. The attractive popular explanation that the name means the 'house of bread' is not historical. David was anointed King of Israel here, but he made Hebron his first capital. After he had taken Jerusalem, and made it his capital, Bethlehem lost importance, serving principally as a market town for Beduin. This occupation has been secondary to its position as a Christian place of pilgrimage.

When Jesus Christ was born, Bethlehem was a place of no importance. Somewhat divergent accounts of his birth are given by St Matthew (2) and by St Luke (2), and these cannot wholly be reconciled. The persecution by Herod and the Flight into Egypt do not belong to the same sequence of events as the Presentation of the Child Jesus in the Temple; St Luke's statement that Our Lady and St Joseph lived in Nazareth, returning there when their business in Bethlehem was done, hardly accords with St Matthew's statement that they were visited in their house in Bethlehem by the Magi, and would have returned there from Egypt had it not been that they were in fear of Herod Archelaus, and so went to Nazareth.

Writing c.155-160 St Justin Martyr, a native of Nablus, regards the location of the Nativity in Bethlehem as a generally accepted belief, and is the first to say that it took place in a cave, a statement reinforced independently by Origen in 248:

In Bethlehem you are shown the cave where he was born, and within the cave the manger where he was wrapped in swaddling clothes. These things that they show you are recognized in the district, even by those who do not share our faith. They admit, that is, that the Jesus whom Christians adore was born in this cave.

Yet Saints Matthew and Luke say nothing about a cave. St Matthew speaks of a house, while St Luke says that the child was laid in a manger because the inn was full.

Somewhat later, at the end of the fourth century, St Jerome says that the Emperor Hadrian set up a shrine of Cybele and Adonis to overshadow Bethlehem. No other writer reports this. If true, Hadrian did the same in Bethlehem as he certainly did in the Holy Sepulchre (below, p. 92), when he made a pagan shrine above it. It is thus reasonable to presume that, acting as he did in AD 135, he was acting on information received, and that the sites that he devoted to pagan worship were those he knew for certain to be those venerated as holy by Christians. St Jerome recounts it as follows:

For the space of about 180 years, from Hadrian's time until the reign of Constantine, the image of Jupiter was venerated on the site of the Resurrection, and a statue of Venus on Golgotha . . . Bethlehem, which now belongs to us . . . was overshadowed by the grove of Tammuz, that is Adonis, and in the cave where the Christ-child once cried they wept for Venus's lover' (Ep.58.3).

23

Even a century later there were pagan idols in front of the Christian church. But, in view of all the reports, the authenticity of the site of the Nativity of Jesus Christ would seem beyond reasonable doubt.

The very dull square in front of the Church of the Nativity was once a colonnaded atrium, some of whose columns are visible in the garden of the Franciscans on the left. On the right are the massive fortress-like walls of the Armenian monastery. These and a huge buttress now mask two of the three doorways which once led into the vestibule, or narthex, of the church. The remaining doorway has been reduced in size several times, finally either in Turkish or Mamluk times. The narthex has been sub-divided, and part is used as a police guard room. In this formerly was a mosaic of the Nativity and the visit of the Magi, which in 614 deceived the Persians into believing that Christians venerate Zoroaster, so that they left the church alone. The inner doorway still has the remains of carvings done by the Armenians in 1227.

The original church, begun by the Empress Helena in 327, no longer survives. It was complete by 333, and rich with gold and silver ornaments, marble, frescoes and mosaics, embroideries, and jewelled lamps and vessels. The clay manger had been replaced by a silver replica. Excavations revealed the ground plan in 1934. It had a nave and four aisles terminating in an octagon, in whose centre an open space looked down into the cave of the Nativity. All that remains of this church is its mosaic floor, parts of which can be viewed through wooden trap doors in the present church.

In 529 the Samaritans revolted. Jerusalem suffered greatly. No written record exists of the destruction at Bethlehem, but a thick layer of ashes and debris found in 1934 showed that Helena's church was destroyed by fire. The present building was constructed under the Emperor Justinian (527-65). Broadly it followed the earlier pattern, but the octagon was replaced by the present choir and apse, and by apsidal transepts. The colonnades were entirely rebuilt, a narthex added, and the atrium moved farther west. Two entrances to the cave were now built, and the church assumed its present shape (see plan 3). On the north side of the church the Crusaders built a convent for Augustinian canons, and in 1101 Baldwin, the first King of Jerusalem, was crowned in Bethlehem by the Patriarch. The church was paved with white marble, its walls decorated with mosaic, and roofed with lead. This seems to have been in some disrepair, for between 1161 and 1169 the

4. Herod's Tomb, Jerusalem

5. Damascus Gate, Jerusalem (at night)

church was restored by the Bishop of Bethlehem, an Englishman named Raoul, who was largely responsible for the surviving mosaics. The marbles in the church and in the cave were either relaid or renewed. It was not until 1266 that Latin Christians were expelled from Bethlehem by the Mamluk Sultan Baybars (1260-77). The Augustinian Canons were forced to flee; their organ, twelve bells from their carillon, and a number of sacred vessels and other objects found under the present Franciscan convent are now to be seen in the Flagellation Museum in Jerusalem. Although in 1347 the Franciscans regained a Latin footing in the church, Bethlehem was then in decline and the church slowly decayed; it was not until 1480 that minimum repairs were put in hand. Wood came from Venice, lead was supplied by King Edward IV of England, and Philip, Duke of Burgundy, supplied craftsmen and other materials. In 1517 the church was looted by the Ottoman Turks, who stripped it of its marble. By 1670 the church was again in disrepair, and this time the Greek Orthodox took the initiative. By 1671 there was a new roof, a splendid iconastasis and other new decorations. Further repairs were needed in 1842, while in 1869 a serious fire destroyed the hangings and other furnishings of the cave of the Nativity. The church is today much as it was left after structural repairs had been carried out by W.E. Harvey in 1934.

The upper church is shared between the Armenians and the Greek Orthodox, the decorations of the former prevailing.

The Cave of the Nativity can be entered from both transepts. A third entrance, from the west, is kept locked, as it was in medieval times. The entrances from the transepts have stairs that date from the Emperor Justinian's rebuilding. Their bronze doors are possibly from that date. The interior, partly rock and partly masonry, has probably been altered by man. Entering from the north, the place of the Nativity is in the left, where there is a small apse containing an altar belonging to the Greeks. Under it is a star inscribed:

HIC DE VIRGINE MARIA JESUS CHRISTUS NATUS EST – 1717
*(Here Jesus Christ was born of the Virgin Mary – 1717)*

The date is that of an earlier silver star placed there by the Latins. It nevertheless disappeared mysteriously in 1847, and was replaced by the present silver star given by the Ottoman Sultan in 1852. In the semi-dome of the apse is the only remaining twelfth century mosaic

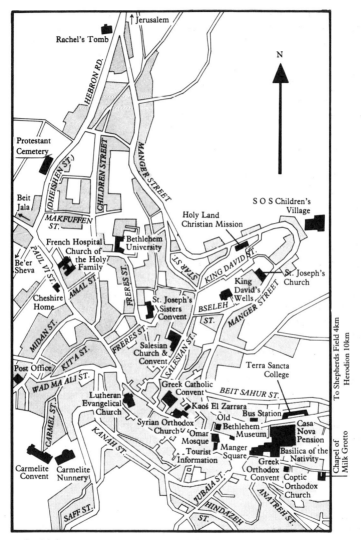

Rachel's Tomb

↑ Jerusalem

N

HEBRON RD.

Protestant
Cemetery

Beit
Jala

(DHEISHEN ST.)

CHILDREN STREET

MANGER STREET

MAKFUFFEN
ST.

Be'er
Sheva

PAUL VI ST.

French Hospital
Church of
the Holy
Family

Bethlehem
University

Holy Land
Christian Mission

S O S Children's
Village

AMAL ST.

Cheshire
Home

FRERES ST.

STAR ST.

KING DAVID ST.

King
David's
Wells

St. Joseph's
Church

St. Joseph's
Sisters
Convent

BSELEH
ST.

MANGER STREET

MIDAN ST.

FRERES ST.

SALESIAN ST.

Salesian
Church &
Convent

Terra Sancta
College

Post Office

KIT'A ST.

WAD MA ALI ST.

Greek Catholic
Convent

BEIT SAHUR ST.

To Shepherds Field 4km
Herodion 10km

Lutheran
Evangelical
Church

Kaoś El Zarrara

Bus Station

CARMEL ST.

KANAH ST.

Syrian Orthodox
Church

'Omar
Mosque

Old
Bethlehem
Museum

Casa
Nova
Pension

Tourist
Information

Manger
Square

Basilica of the
Nativity

Chapel of
Milk Grotto

Carmelite
Convent

Carmelite
Nunnery

Greek
Orthodox
Convent

Coptic
Orthodox
Church

JUBAIA ST.

SAFF ST.

HINDA'ZEH
ST.

ANATREH ST.

2. Bethlehem

decoration in the cave. A contemporary pilgrim, Johannes Phocas, described it as it was then:

In the apse is figured the Virgin reclining upon her bed . . . as she looks at her infant. Beyond her are the ox and the ass, the manger and the babe, and the company of shepherds in whose ears the voice of heaven rang . . .

Phocas also mentions that it included the Magi arriving with their gifts, but omits another scene, still partly visible, the Washing of the Child. The words PAX HOMINIBUS – Peace towards men – from the Angels' song, can also be read.

On the south side of the cave is the Chapel of the Manger, a rock shelf covered with marble slabs. Originally in Constantine's church it was of silver. St Jerome wrote:

Oh that I might see that Manger where the Lord lay! Now we, as honouring Christ, have taken away that clay Manger and set in its place a silver one; but I prize more that which is taken away.

This, and the Altar of the Magi opposite, are under the guardianship of the Franciscans.

Upstairs access to the Church of St Catherine of Alexandria, built by the Franciscans in 1884, is reached through a small door in the northern apse. West of it is the medieval cloister of the Augustinian Canons. On the south side of this church a door leads to a staircase to a series of caves which connect with the Cave of the Nativity. The first chapel is that of the Holy Innocents, and a deep cave can be seen through a hole in the floor. South of this, at a higher level, is the Chapel of St Joseph, ascribed to the seventeenth century. A passage on the left leading out of the Chapel of the Holy Innocents leads to the tomb and Chapel of St Jerome, where traditionally he translated the Vulgate, the official Latin version of the Bible. An altar on the right side of the passage is dedicated to St Eusebius of Cremona, St Jerome's successor as superior of his monastery. Another altar on the opposite side of the chapel covers

*II. Upper Church and Buildings.* 11. Stairs to crypts. 12. Latin Church of St. Catherine. 13. Cloister. 14. Franciscan Monastery. 15. Nave. 16. Baptismal Font. 17. Entrance to Armenian Monastery. 18. Armenian Monastery. 19. Greek Garden. 20. Greek Monastery. 21. Chapel of the Armenians. 22. Statue of the Blessed Virgin Mary.

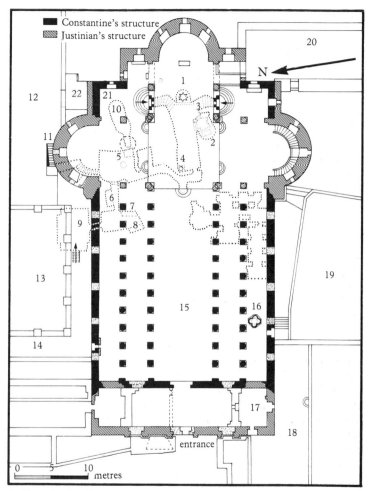

## 3. Church of the Nativity, Bethlehem

*I. Crypts.* 1. Altar of the Nativity. 2. Altar of the Manger. 3. Altar of the Three Kings. 4. Well of the Star. 5. Altar of the Holy Innocents. 6. Altar of St. Eusebius. 7. Altar of SS. Paula and Eustochium. 8. Altar of St. Jerome. 9. Cell of St. Jerome. 10. Crypt of the Holy Innocents.

the tomb of St Jerome's associates, Saints Paula and Eustochium.

*The Shepherds' Fields* In the valley east of Bethlehem, reached by a twisting motor road, but in fact only 1100 yards (1015 metres) is the village of Beit Sahur. 500 yards east of the village (460 metres) is the Greek Orthodox Church covering a cave with a fourth century mosaic floor. It has been reopened recently. 1100 yards (1015 metres) farther north is a Franciscan church consecrated in 1954, on the site of a fourth century monastery, and labelled CAMPO DEI PASTORI (Shepherds' Field).

*Herodion (Har Hordos)* About 6¼ miles (10 km.) south-east of Bethlehem is a palace citadel built by Herod the Great between 24 and 15 BC. The exterior resembles an extinct volcano, but it is in fact of sandstone. The interior is circular, and resembles Roman imperial tombs. There are three half towers and one complete round tower, in which Herod is believed to be buried. The living quarters were small, and Herod cannot have been accompanied, if he used it, by much of an entourage. At some uncertain date it was used as a Byzantine monastery, and there are the remains of a small chapel. The motor road stops half way up the hill, and then a short, rough track reaches a staircase of forty-three steps. The place is worth a visit from Bethlehem chiefly because of the superb view, extending as far as the Dead Sea on a clear day.

6. Jerusalem to Jericho Road

# ITINERARY II

## *Jerusalem to Nazareth*

There are three routes from Jerusalem to Nazareth, the shortest, via Ramallah, Shekhem and Nablus, and passing near the ancient Sebastiya (Samaria), being the most interesting and picturesque (136 km.). A longer route is via Jericho and Jordan Valley. Both of these routes are to be avoided in times of unrest, but generally can be traversed by Arab taxis. A third route is via Latrun, Ramla, Tulkarm and Afula, passing the crossroads of Megiddo (169 km., 105 miles). There are two buses daily from the Egged Bus Station, and also a twice daily communal (*cherut*) taxi service from the Nablus Road (current price single 20 shekels per person each way), close to the Convent of the Franciscan White Sisters. Places in the taxi service should be booked in advance to avoid disappointment, but can often be obtained at short notice in the early morning service, at 5 a.m., which carries the mail to Nazareth. The time taken is approximately 2½ hours.

The evangelists do not agree where Mary and Joseph lived before Jesus' birth. Matt.2 implies that it was Bethlehem, but Luke 2.4-5 says it was Nazareth. A strong tradition places the birth of Our Lady in Jerusalem (below, p.112), where she was related to Zacharias, a priest whose service in the Temple necessitated his residence in the Holy City. Luke 1.39-40 relates her visit to his wife Elizabeth when she was reported to be with child, a journey she appears to have made alone. Traditionally this is sited at Ain Karim (below, p.39), but it is not very plausible to suggest that she would have travelled, herself a young Jewish girl in child, the long three day journey from Nazareth to Ain Karim alone. When the Holy Family returned from Egypt, it was to Nazareth that they went for fear of Herod Archelaus. Thenceforward it was Jesus' home town (Matt.13.54, Luke 4.16), where they had relatives (Matt. 13.54). As late as AD 249 St Conon, at his trial before his martyrdom, declared that he was born at Nazareth in Galilee and that he belonged to the family of the Lord, to whom a cult had been offered from the time of his ancestors.

The present town of Nazareth has a population of about 40,000, about half Christian and half Muslim. Above the town is the modern

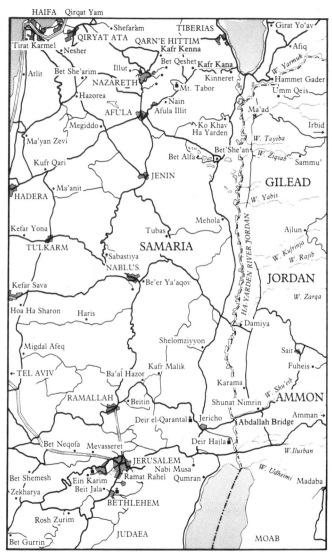

4. Jerusalem to Nazareth

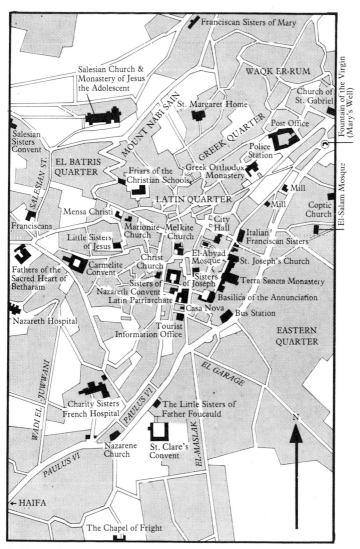

Franciscan Sisters of Mary

Salesian Church &
Monastery of Jesus
the Adolescent

WAQK ER-RUM

MOUNT NABI SA'IN

St. Margaret Home

Church of
St. Gabriel

Salesian
Sisters
Convent

GREEK QUARTER

Post Office

Police
Station

Fountain of the Virgin
(Mary's Well)

EL BATRIS
QUARTER

Friars of the
Christian Schools

Greek Orthodox
Monastery

SALESIAN ST.

Mill

LATIN QUARTER

Mill

Coptic
Church

Mensa Christi

City
Hall

El-Salam Mosque

Franciscans

Marionite
Church

Melkite
Church

Italian
Franciscan Sisters

Little Sisters
of Jesus

Christ
Church

El-Abyad
Mosque

St. Joseph's Church

Fathers of the
Sacred Heart of
Betharam

Carmelite
Convent

Sisters of
Nazareth Convent

Sisters
of Joseph

Terra Sancta Monastery

Latin Patriarchate

Basilica of the Annunciation

Casa Nova

Bus Station

Nazareth Hospital

Tourist
Information Office

EASTERN
QUARTER

EL GARAGE

WADI EL JUWANI

PAULUS VI

Charity Sisters
French Hospital

The Little Sisters of
Father Foucauld

N

PAULUS VI

Nazarene
Church

St. Clare's
Convent

EL-MASLAK

← HAIFA

The Chapel of Fright

5. Nazareth

Jewish township of Nazerat Illit. There are numerous churches and chapels, but only five buildings of any antiquity. Nazareth was not an early centre of pilgrimage, nor did Constantine erect a basilica there when he had those of the Holy Sepulchre and the Nativity built by his mother. He only gave permission to one Joseph of Tiberias to build a church there. Nazareth had a bishop by 460, but it is not until 570 that Anonymous of Piacenza speaks of a basilica of 'the house of the Blessed Virgin Mary.' Arculf (670) is the first to connect the site with the Annunciation, which he, and other pilgrims, place, not in a grotto, but in a stone-built house.

There are no traces of Joseph of Tiberias' church remaining. Excavations begun in 1955 disclosed a Byzantine church of the first half of the fifth century, which did not include the Grotto of the Annunciation. Al-Mas'udi saw it in 943, but it appears to have been demolished at the beginning of the eleventh century, perhaps by the Caliph al-Hakim in 1009, or by one of the Seljuq Turks. The Crusaders found it in ruins in 1102, and built a cathedral there, which was complete by 1106. This incorporated the ruined Byzantine church, and was 81 yards long and 32½ wide, with three apses at the east end. The Grotto of the Annunciation lay under its north aisle. The basilica was destroyed by the Mamluk Sultan Baybars in 1263, but the grotto itself was unharmed. The buildings lay in ruins until 1730, when the Franciscans obtained a *firman* from the Ottoman Sultan, which allowed them only six months in which to construct a new church. This, a comparatively small building, was built in the manner of the *martyria* in the churches in Rome, the principal altar being raised on a balcony built across the top of the grotto, leaving it exposed to view. This church was only 23 yards long and 16 wide (21m. x 14·7m), and incapable of serving the needs of the thousands of pilgrims that the air age has brought to Nazareth. Accordingly demolition began in 1955, enabling the whole site to be investigated archaeologically. The new church was then built, with a pilgrimage shrine at ground level, incorporating the remains of earlier buildings, and a large church in the upper story to accommodate large pilgrimages.

In the centre of the underground church is the apse of the fifth century Byzantine church. In front is a basin 2 metres (approx. 2½ yards) square considered by the excavators to be a pre-Constantinian baptistery because of its shape and the graffiti on its plastered walls. It

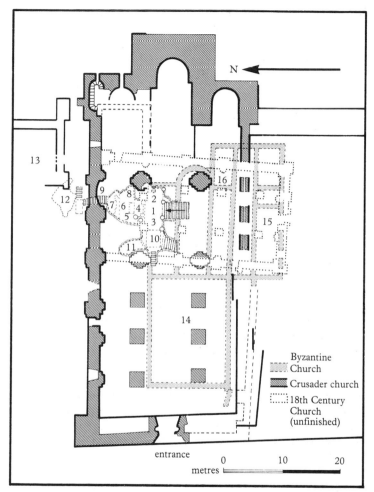

## 6(a). The Church of the Annunciation

1. Chapel of the Angel. 2. Altar of Sts. Joachim and Anna. 3. Altar of St. Gabriel. 4. Gabriel's pillar. 5. Mary's Pillar. 6. Altar of the Annunciation. 7. North Apse (old chapel of St. Joseph). 8. East apse (oldest site of the Annunciation). 9. Franciscan staircase. 10. Mosaic of Conon. 11. Grave of Joseph? 12. Kitchen of Mary. 13. Exit to yard leading to the Monastery and Church of St. Joseph. 14. Atrium (Byzantine). 15. Convent (Byzantine). 16. Sacristy (Byzantine).

was found sealed under a mosaic. Other remains of this period lie outside the north wall of the Crusader church; stores, granaries, oil presses and the foundations of dwellings. On the left of the basin a short flight of stairs leads to a mosaic floor inscribed: 'Gift of Conon, a deacon of Jerusalem.' Behind the Byzantine apse is the triple twelfth century apse and a staircase. In the south apse six elegant capitals are to be seen. Apparently they were never used for the Crusader church for which they were intended. Forty-eight figurines depict scenes from the lives of the apostles. They are of northern French origin. The altar of the Annunciation is a seventeenth century one, inscribed: VERBUM CARO HIC FACTUM EST (Here the Word was made flesh). Below it is a marble plaque venerated by pilgrims as the place in which Our Lady stood. Roman columns stand in front of this altar, brought from either Caesarea or Sephoris.

The upper church is reached by a staircase in the northwest corner. Crossing it to the north one reaches a courtyard, with the Church of St Joseph on the north side. It is built on the foundations seen plainly outside in the lowest courses of the walls of a Crusader church, which was completed in 1914. In medieval French Romanesque style, it is of a refreshing simplicity. The first mention of it occurs in the work of the Franciscan Quaresmius (1616-26) as 'the house and workshop of Joseph'. Matt.13.55 calls Jesus the carpenter's son, and Mark 6.3 calls Jesus himself a carpenter, but the Greek word *tekton* can mean a man who works in wood, stone or metal. In a treeless country Joseph could not have been a joiner in our sense of the word. Wood was imported only for ploughs and yokes, and wooden tables have been found in Jerusalem only. There is no mention of a workshop before c.1620, when it would have appeared to have arisen from popular sentiment. Since 1914 the church has been known also as the Church of the Nutrition, as the place where Jesus was brought up.

Excavations under the church have revealed a cave system, including four silos, three cisterns for storing water, and what has been identified as a baptismal font with seven steps leading down into it. It seems to have been built out of an earlier silo. There are carefully planned air ducts to keep the place fresh. There is also the remains of a mosaic from a building no longer in existence. The excavators interpret the system as a baptismal complex belonging to the Judaeo-Christians.

Up the street almost due east of St Joseph's Church is the Greek

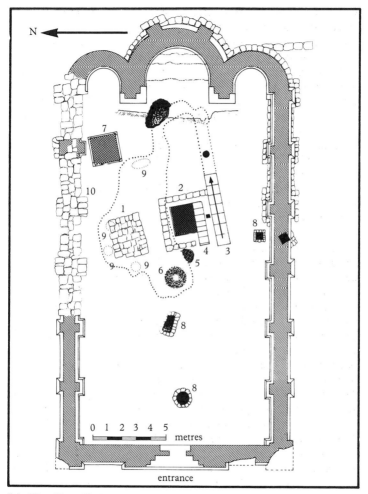

## (b). The Church of St. Joseph

1. Base of former pillar. 2. Baptismal tank. 3. Staircase and underground passage cut into the rock and leading into the grotto. 4. Stairs leading to first Baptismal tank. 5. Remains of a building now destroyed. 6. Vents for light and air. 7. Second baptismal tank. 8. Cisterns. The one closest to the baptismal tank is contemporary with it and was intended to keep baptismal water in reserve. 9. Silos. 10. Remains of former buildings.

Catholic Church known as the Synagogue Church. It is believed to be on the site of the ancient synagogue where Jesus preached (Luke 4.28-9).

To the north of the town is the Greek Orthodox Church of St Gabriel, and adjacent to it Mary's Well. The latter is filled from a spring 162 yards away by a conduit. It is venerated because this water would have been used by the Holy Family, and is led into the church by a stone duct. The church in its present state is a seventeenth century construction over the remains of three former churches. By the north wall of the crypt is the well, with an Arabic inscription: 'Annunciation of the Virgin and Well of Water,' thus locating the Annunciation there. Certainly there was a Byzantine church here in the sixth century, and one of considerable size in Crusader times. The church first received the name of St Gabriel in 1187; it was only after 1600 that the name Mary's Well was attributed to it.

7.   The Church of the Annunciation, Nazareth

# ITINERARY III

## *The Ministry of St John Baptist*

The Gospels do not give any precise details about the location of events in the life of St John Baptist, but there are a number of sites at which they are commemorated, and which are not inconsonant with the Gospel story.

*Ain Karim* (locally Ein Kerem) lies 5 miles (8 km) west of Jerusalem. There are frequent buses from the Jaffa Gate, the Damascus Gate and from the Central Bus Station (see map 1).

Ain Karim is the traditional site of the Visitation of Our Lady to St Elizabeth (Luke 1.39), the birth of St John, and close to one of the sites commemorating his sojourn in the wilderness. Until 1948 it was largely a Muslim village with only 300 Christians, but since 1948 it has undergone a complete change, and is inhabited almost exclusively by Jews. There are a number of Latin and Russian Orthodox establishments, but the only ones of antiquity are as below.

The Church of St John Baptist is at the bottom of the valley as one enters, up a lane on the right. It is built over the remains of a fifth century church which the Crusaders reconstructed, and which was destroyed after their departure. The present building was completed in 1674. On the left a staircase leads to the grotto of the Nativity of St John. To the right of the church a door leads to the remains of the Crusader buildings. During excavations in 1885 while building the present porch on the west side two rock tombs were found, which have been thought to hold the remains of the Holy Innocents, as described by Epiphanius. South of this another chapel was discovered in 1941-2, with a mosaic floor, over a press of the Roman period.

Crossing the valley to the Church of the Visitation one passes what has been known as the Virgin's Fountain since the fourteenth century. The church itself is of two storeys, completed only in 1955, and is reached up a steep path. Archaeological investigation has disclosed pre-Roman and Roman remains, a Hellenistic tomb, a Byzantine reservoir, and a grotto with a cistern round which the Crusaders erected a church. The movement of the family from one site to another is perhaps to be explained as a flight after the Massacre of the Innocents. The

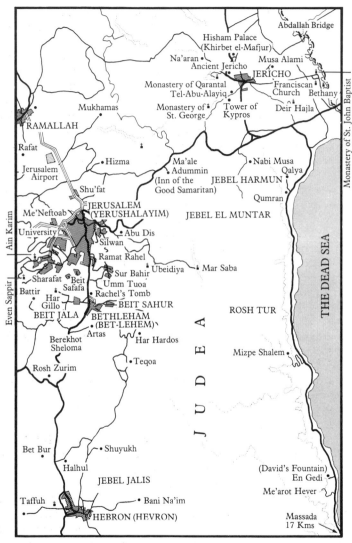

7. Jerusalem to Jericho and the Dead Sea

veneration of the sites where the *Magnificat* and the *Benedictus* were first uttered seems to have followed. The church has a superbly kept garden, and is a wonderful place of peace and quiet.

*Desert of St John.* Returning to the centre of Ain Karim, we turn left down a road which joins the Jaffa-Tel Aviv road at Eshtaol. After 1½ miles (2 km.) a road on the left leads to Even Sapir. At the first house on the right a rough track leads to the Greek Melkite Monastery. Cars, taxis and buses must be left at the top, because, although the track is motorable, it is never broad enough for a vehicle to turn round.

A chapel and convent here were erected by the Franciscans in 1922, as commemorated by a large Latin inscription at the entrance gate. There are vestiges of a twelfth century monastic building, all over a grotto with a spring known as Ain al-Habis (Spring of the Hermit), where St John is believed to have lived in seclusion. Higher up the hill is a building belonging to Huguenot Sisters of the same order as that of Taizé. A small chapel contains a tomb, now empty, under an apse, said to have been that of St Elizabeth. It is possibly of Byzantine origin. This is a retreat house, and permission is needed for entry.

An alternative site for the seclusion of St John in the desert has been proposed by Fr Clemens Kopp, 5 miles (8 km.) west of Hebron at Taffuh, where, in a deep narrow valley to the south-west, are the ruins of a well still known as *Ain al-Ma'mudiyyah*, the Well of Baptism. Buildings belonging to a church and a monastery have been identified here as belonging to the reign of Justinian (527-65).

*St John the Baptist in the Jordan Valley.* There are bus services to Jericho hourly from 6.45 a.m. until 5.00 p.m., and to the Dead Sea, Qumran, Ein Gedi, Massada and Zohar at frequent intervals from 8.30 a.m. until 4.30 p.m. Visitors should be prepared for a very rapid change of temperature: there can be a difference of 40° Fahrenheit (5° Centigrade) between Jerusalem and Jericho. The Dead Sea is 1317 feet (405 metres) below sea level, making a total drop of 4017 feet (1436 metres) from Jerusalem. Hats and sunglasses are advisable.

The evangelists place St John Baptist's mission in the wilderness near the Jordan. One road down to Jericho was constructed in Roman times, and is still walkable. A Turkish road with numerous hairpin bends was replaced by the Jordanian Government by a modern road completed only in 1964. At 11¼ miles (18 km.) down the modern road are some ancient walls known as the Inn of the Good Samaritan. There

41

are fragments of (?) a Byzantine monastery which also served as a caravanserai, reconstructed as a Turkish Police Post in 1903. At 17½ miles (28 km.) the road forks, and on the left a road leads down the Wadi al-Qilt to the Greek Monastery of Saints John and George of Koziba, founded in the sixth century. It is reached by a flight of 300 steps. At 17 miles (27 km.) a road to the right leads to Nabi Musa (Nebi Moussa), where in 1269 Sultan Baybars of Egypt built a mosque and tomb chamber in honour of Moses. It has no historical foundation.

The Dead Sea is now reached on the right, 792 metres (2574 feet) below sea level. On the left is the plain of Jericho and the river Jordan. It is part of the Great Rift Valley which extends from Lake Houleh in the north down through to Kenya and Tanzania. Round Jericho is a well-watered region, but south of it is a desolation of scrub where the Jordan flows through often grotesquely shaped hills into the Dead Sea. The river mouth is only 68 miles (109 km.) from Lake Tiberias, but the river winds so much that it travels 187 miles (299 km.). In former times there were fords across it at the Abdallah Bridge (formerly known as the Allenby Bridge); the only crossing today into the Kingdom of Jordan. About 4½ miles (7 km.) south is the Greek Monastery of St John Baptist, regarded by some as the place of Christ's Baptism by St John. On the opposite side of the road is the Franciscan enclosure, with a small building known as the Little Temple at the Piace of the Baptism. A church already existed here in the fifth century, and was succeeded by a number of others, most of them destroyed by earthquakes, the last in 1956. The most recent dates from that year. 5/8 mile (1 km.) farther on, near the springs of Wadi Kharar remains of Byzantine buildings are said to mark the site of Bethany beyond Jordan, where John preached and baptized (John 1.28).

The Gospels give somewhat abrupt information about his preaching and baptism, to which 'there went out to him Jerusalem and all Judaea, and all the country about Jordan'. His baptism by immersion was for those determined to produce 'fruits worthy of penance' in order to face the forthcoming Last Judgement (Luke 3.8), and in this way it differed from the initiation into Judaism of the baptism of proselytes and the frequent purifications of the Essenes and other Jewish sects (see below, p.44). At the baptism of Jesus John the Baptist proclaimed him as the Lamb of God . . . who takes away the sin of the world, and, next day at Bethany, a group of disciples formed round Jesus (John 1.35-42). This

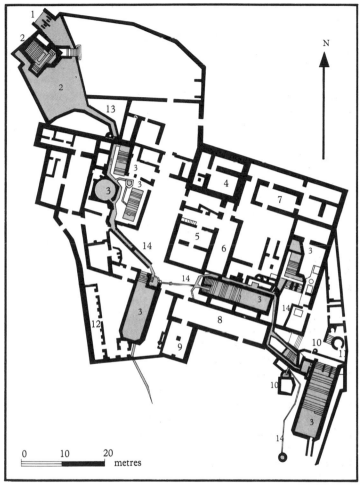

## 8. Qumran

1. Aqueduct Entrance. 2. Reservoirs. 3. Reservoirs. 4. Watch tower. 5. Room with benches along the walls. 6. Scriptorium. 7. Kitchen. 8. Assembly hall & refectory. 9. Pantry. 10. Potters' workshops. 11. Kilns. 12. Cattle byres. 13. Conduit. 14. Conduits.

Bethany is not to be confused with the Bethany of Lazarus (below, pp.57-8).

These sites, and the site of Herod's castle-palace at Machaerus, where Herod Antipas had the Baptist done to death, lie in the frontier region between Israeli occupied territory on the West Bank and the Kingdom of Jordan, Machaerus itself being on the east bank. They can only be approached by permission of the authorities.

*Qumran, and the Finding of the Dead Sea Scrolls.* Khirbeh (the ruin of) Qumran lies on the main road 7 miles (11 km.) south of Jericho on the west side of the Dead Sea. It was the centre of an Essene community, an austere esoteric Jewish sect. Its members lived a monastic life, from c.150 BC until AD 68, in cliff caves, tents and underground chambers. They gathered only for ritual purifications and ritual meals, and the copying of the scriptures and devotional and religious works. There was an Israelite fort here in the eighth century BC, possibly the 'city of salt' of Joshua 15.61-2. For unexplained reasons, during the reign of John Hyrcanus (134-103 BC) the community increased to 200, when extensive building took place. This was damaged by an earthquake in 31 BC. The community abandoned the site, but returned some thirty years later, remaining until it was expelled by the Romans in AD 68.

Ritual purification with water was an essential part of Essene practice. The elaborate system of dams and aqueducts, decantation pools and cisterns, confusing to the visitor, (see plan 8) can best be seen from the tower in the middle of the site. This was the salient feature of the main building, with a central courtyard, a refectory and/or assembly hall with a pantry, kitchen, common room, scriptorium, potter's workshop and cattle pen. Ritual meals, unique in character so far as is known, took place, the remains of animal bones, sheep and goats, and less commonly cows and calves, being carefully buried. Between 1947 and 1952 in adjacent caves large quantities of manuscripts were found in scroll form, of the Hebrew Scriptures, and of orthodox Jewish and Essene devotional and religious works. These amount to more than 40,000 documents, and are still being studied. The main collection is housed in the Shrine of the Book adjacent to the Israel Museum, in a separate building of dramatic appearance.

46 miles (74 km.) further on is Massada, the great Herodian stronghold of Herod the Great, first fortified by Alexander Jannaeus (103 BC to 76 BC).

## *Jesus in Galilee*

It is not possible to reconstruct with accuracy all the movements of the ministry of Jesus in Galilee. His activity occurred chiefly on the shores of the Lake of Galilee (also Lake Gennesareth, and Lake Tiberias), with Capharnaum as the principal base. Almost all of them lie along the line of the road from Nazareth to the town of Tiberias, and then along the lakeside.

There are local buses along these routes; inquiry as to their times may be made from the Government Information Centre in Nazareth. Taxis are also available there and in Tiberias.

The ministry of Jesus began soon after John the Baptist had been imprisoned (Mark 1.14 and parallels). A first miracle was performed at *Cana in Galilee*, usually identified as Kafr Kenna, 4 miles (6½ km.) along the road to Tiberias. Cana today is a town of 8,000 inhabitants, of whom 2,500 are Christians, and the rest Muslims. The lower levels of the Franciscan church here have Roman remains thought to date before the fourth century, in addition to Byzantine and Crusader remains. It is thought to be on the site of a third century synagogue. The site was acquired by the Franciscans in 1641, and the present church built in 1879. In the adjacent Greek Orthodox Church is shown an earthenware jar said to have been used on the occasion of the miracle of turning the water into wine, and similar jars were also shown in the middle ages. 8½ miles (13½ km.) north of Nazareth is Khirbet Kana, an uninhabited mound of ruins, where there is also a Franciscan church, formerly a mosque. Apparently a synagogue stood here c.AD 500. The present church was built in 1883, and an inscription records the place in which stood six water pots: HIC ERANT SEX HYDRIAE POSITAE. Be this as it may, it seems unlikely that a synagogue could have been constructed on a site known at an early period to be sacred to Christians. Nevertheless the site of Khirbet Kana has been preferred to Kafr Kenna by many pilgrims.

*Jacob's Well.* After the wedding in Cana Jesus visited Jerusalem (John 2.14-22), and then spent some time in Judaea (Jn.3.22), following which the opposition of the Pharisees forced him to retreat via

Samaria to Galilee. Jacob's Well (John.4.7-29), where a Samaritan woman drew water and conversed with Jesus, is more easily visited in Itinerary V (below, p.57).

*Tiberias.* The town, mentioned incidentally in the Gospels, is not associated with any event in the life of Jesus. Boats leave the quay for trips on the lake at frequent intervals. The surface of the lake is 681 feet (209 metres) below the level of the Mediterranean, and 13 miles (21 km.) long and 6 miles (9·5 km.) at its widest. The road runs north along the west side of the lake in the direction of Capharnaum.

*Magdala.* Now known as El Mejdel, the village that gave Mary Magdalen (Luke 8.2) her name, lies 3 miles (5 km.) north of Tiberias. At *Ginnosar* 1½ m. (2½ km.) the Kibbutz houses a first century boat, found in 1986, of the type the disciples probably used.

*Bethsaida*, over which Jesus lamented (Matt.11.21), the native village of Peter, Andrew and Philip, is generally placed at Khirbet el-Minyeh, about 4 miles (6·4 km.) north of Magdala. After 1 mile (1·6 km.) one reaches Tabhga, the modern Arabic name representing the Greek *Heptapegon*, the place of seven springs. Three churches commemorate the Beatitudes, the Multiplication of the Loaves and Fishes and the Apparition of the Risen Christ to the Apostles, known also as the Church of the Primacy of St. Peter.

*The Church of the Beatitudes* is reached by a track from the north side of the main road, and is taken care of by Franciscan Sisters, who maintain an adjacent hospice. It was built to commemorate the Sermon on the Mount in 1938, and is a building of exquisite beauty and proportions. The view of the lake from it is superb. Not far away are the remains of the fourth century Chapel of the Sermon on the Mount, with part of a mosaic surviving. This can now be seen in Capharnaum. The building was of rough-hewn basalt, the most common material available in the locality. There was also a small monastery here.

*The Church of the Multiplication of the Loaves and Fishes* is located on the east side of the road. There was already a church here in 384, which was replaced in the fifth century by a basilica and a convent. The basilica had a large open courtyard decorated with mosaics. A narthex led into a cruciform church, with three aisles. The apse and presbytery contained an altar with a stone on which Jesus placed one of the loaves. The whole church and its sacristies were covered with mosaics, which included birds and animals represented with great elegance.

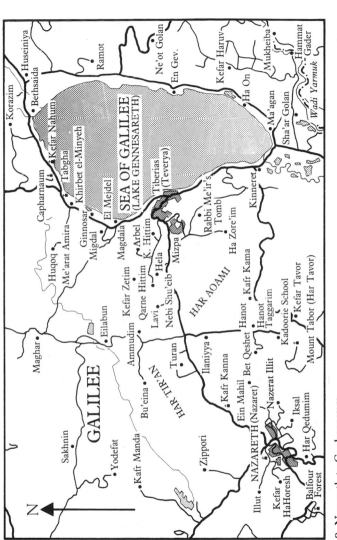

9. Nazareth to Capharnaum

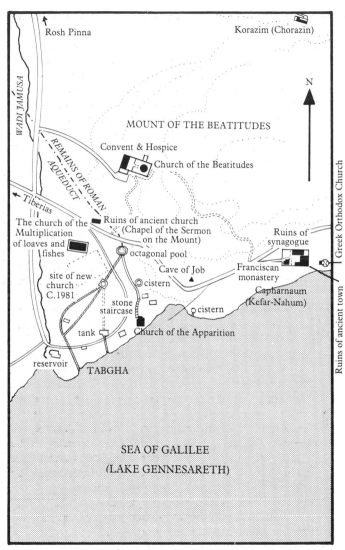

Rosh Pinna

Korazim (Chorazin)

WADI JAMUSA

REMAINS OF ROMAN AQUEDUCT

← Tiberias

N

MOUNT OF THE BEATITUDES

Convent & Hospice

Church of the Beatitudes

Greek Orthodox Church

The church of the Multiplication of loaves and fishes

Ruins of ancient church (Chapel of the Sermon on the Mount)

octagonal pool

Cave of Job

Ruins of synagogue

site of new church C.1981

cistern

Franciscan monastery

stone staircase

cistern

Capharnaum (Kefar-Nahum)

tank

Church of the Apparition

reservoir

TABGHA

Ruins of ancient town

SEA OF GALILEE
(LAKE GENNESARETH)

10. Tabgha and the vicinity

There are seven mills in the vicinity and a number of cisterns (see plan 10).

On the lake shore itself is the *Church of the Apparition of the Risen Christ to the Apostles*, in which the Primacy of Peter is commemorated. The small chapel, built by the Franciscans in 1933, lies beside the lake shore. On the main site a large church has recently been built by German Benedictines, following a visit by Pope Paul VI on 5 January 1964, when he expressed a wish for a more worthy monument. Here (John.21) Christ had conferred the Primacy upon Peter. The rocky steps referred to by Egeria in 384 were once visible on the south of the old church; here, she says, Our Lord stood. She does not speak of a church, but it is claimed that one was built here by the Empress Helena. Here in the ninth century Twelve Thrones (Luke 22.20) were shown, and the bases of six pairs of columns can be seen when the lake is low. The church was destroyed c.1187, repaired about 1260, and razed to the ground in 1263. The steps were bull-dozed in 1970.

*Capharnaum* is 1 mile (1·6 km.) farther on from Tabgha. Excavations of part of the ancient town were carried out by Fr V. Corbo in 1968-84 under the patronage of the Franciscans and the Italian Government. One enters through a parking lot with a coffee stall through a narrow passage with a modern mosaic pavement. On the right is the Franciscan convent, on the left a garden, with lavatories just beyond. Immediately to the right after this entrance is a ticket office and bookstall. Immediately in front is an Italian garden containing carved masonry removed from the ruins of the synagogue, an oil press, and grindstones. Beyond is the area of the excavations, which fall into five main sections.

The site was first occupied in the late Bronze Age, and then deserted. It was reoccupied in the second century BC. In the first century AD it served as the principal base of the ministry of Christ in Galilee, and was visited by Flavius Josephus during the Jewish Revolt later in the century. Next to the synagogue in which Jesus taught was the house of St Peter, and the latter came to be transformed into a 'house-church' by the Judaeo-Christians who lived side by side with orthodox Jews. It was for this that Rabbi Issi of Caesarea cursed Capharnaum in the following century. In the fourth century the 'house-church' was enlarged, and at the end of the century, an elaborate synagogue was built beside it, in imported white stone. In the fifth century the 'house-church' was absorbed in an octagonal church, which was built above it. This was

49

described by the Anonymous of Piacenza in 570, but in the following century the site was abandoned. Only in the nineteenth century was the synagogue rediscovered, and excavations followed early in the twentieth century. At first it was thought that this surviving synagogue was the actual one in which Jesus had taught, but this was disproved by the later excavations. Documentary evidence and archaeological findings sustain the identification of ruins with the town mentioned in the Gospels and by later pilgrims. Here a number of the apostles received their calling, a number of miracles took place including those of Peter's mother-in-law, the centurion's servant, and Jairus's daughter raised from apparent death. Here too was preached the sermon on the Bread of Life (John.6.25-59). The town extended along the lake shore for some 540 yards (500 m.), with a depth of 270 yards (250 m.). It was hemmed in between the lake and a hill on the western side. The town was divided by lanes into blocks, with the walls of the houses built of basalt and the roofs of dried mud and straw. They had no water supply nor sanitary facilities. The inhabitants made their living by fishing, farming and trade.

Immediately in front on the right is the House of St. Peter. It looks like a tangle of walls. A board shows a plan in different colours differentiating the primitive house, the two stages of the 'house-church', and the final stage of an octagonal church superimposed upon them. The object of this arrangement was because the central room was regarded as especially holy, and, like the Dome of the Rock (below, pp.74-5), it enabled worshippers to venerate and to circumambulate it in a ceremonial manner, as is still done in the Holy Sepulchre in solemn processions (below, pp.98-100). Early pilgrims visited it as the House of St Peter, and inscriptions show that they came to implore the pity and mercy of Christ.

To the left lay the synagogue, evidently with either a gallery or an upper storey for women, and an atrium, or courtyard on the right hand side, built on a raised platform. There was an entry on the north side, three on the south, and one to the courtyard on the west. The prayer hall had colonnades supporting the upper storey. The final stage of the building is dated by fourth to fifth century coins found in the mortar below the paved floor. Some 30,000 coins have been recovered. Beyond the synagogue two blocks of buildings have been exposed, and in all probability it was surrounded by a third block. The ornamentation of

9. Pool of Bethsaida, Jerusalem

8. Street beside the West Wall, Jerusalem

the buildings and its carved stonework is of a high standard, as are also its mosaics.

About 216 yards (200 m.) north of the town is a large mausoleum. Further north, some 2 miles (3·2 km.) away, is the *Chorazin* of the Gospels (Matt.11.21). Two other villages of this name, which means Fish-Village, are across the R. Jordan in Syrian territory, while 22½ miles (36 km.) north of the river mouth is Banias, the former *Caesarea Philippi*, where Peter confessed to Christ, the Son of the living God, and received his commission (Matt.16.13).

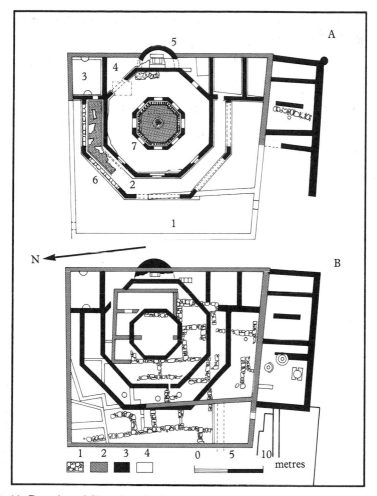

## 11. Remains of Church at Capharnaum

**A. Reconstruction of the plan of the church. c.A.D.450**. 1. Recent wall. 2. Portico. 3. Sacristies and store rooms. 4. Open spaces. 5. Baptistery and font. 6. Remains of mosaic pavement. 7. Mosaic pavement.

**B. The House of St Peter and its development as a church**. *Level 1*. Domestic Buildings. 1st c.B.C. – 4th c.A.D. *Level 2*. Domestic Building modified to provide a house-church in the middle 4th c.AD. *Level 3*. Octagonal church built c.A.D..450 after levelling domestic buildings. *Level 4*. Other later constructions.

10.   The Church of the Beatitudes, Gallilee

# ITINERARY V

## *The Last Journey to Jerusalem*

Although not strictly in sequence, it is convenient to treat the raising from the dead of the widow's son at Nain and the Transfiguration on Mount Tabor in conjunction with Jesus' last journey to Jerusalem. Neither of these places is accessible by bus. They are nevertheless included in tours, and are also accessible by taxi. The ascent of Mount Tabor is precipitous, and not one for an inexperienced driver. Nain lies close to the main road approximately 5 miles (8 km.) north of Afula, and presents no difficulties. Although the topographical indications in the evangelists are by no means clear, it would seem certain that Jesus passed from Galilee to Samaritan country (Luke 9.52-3), and then most likely reached Jerusalem for the feast of the dedication of the Temple in December; and then 'went again beyond Jordan, into that place where John was baptizing first' (John 10.39ff). Only after that did he return to Jerusalem via Bethany and Bethphage. His announcement to his disciples echoes across the ages:

. . . he took the twelve disciples aside, and on the way he said to them, 'Behold, we are going up to Jerusalem; and the Son of Man will be delivered to the chief priests and scribes, and they will condemn him to death, and deliver him up to the Gentiles to be mocked and scourged and crucified, and he will be raised on the third day' (Matt.20.17-19).

The greatest part of the journey lies on the bus route between Nazareth and Jerusalem, and then between Jerusalem and Jericho. It is only possible to follow it in detail by touring coach or by taxi (see map 5).

*Mount Tabor* lies east of Nazareth. To reach it from there the Afula road passes about ½ m. (1 km.) south-west of Kfar Tavor, where a by-road climbs up 5 m. (8 km.) to the top. It is now tarmac all the way. It can also be reached on the way back from Tiberias, turning right after 6¼ miles (10 km.) at Kinneret, then 11¼ miles (18 km.) to Kfar Tavor, then 4⅓ miles (7 km.) to the turn-off up the track a further 4⅓ miles (7 km.), a total of 15 miles (24 km.).

The mount itself is of markedly striking appearance, in shape like a sugar-loaf. It has been inhabited since 80,000 BC. The localization of the Transfiguration on Mount Tabor has fluctuated. Eusebius of Caesarea hesitated between Tabor and Hermon. The Pilgrim of Bordeaux (333) placed it on the Mount of Olives. In 348 Cyril of Jerusalem decided upon Tabor, followed by all the fathers thereafter. In 570 the Anonymous Pilgrim of Piacenza saw three basilicas there, but Willibald saw only one in 724-7. At the foot of the mountain is the village of Dabburiyyah, where tradition locates the cure of the epileptic boy (Luke 9.37-43). The site at the top is divided between Latins and Greeks.

The first turn-off leads to the Greek property. Inside is the Cave of Melchisedek, where he is said to have received Abraham (Gen.14.17-20). Farther on is the Franciscan property, surrounded by a fortress built by Saladin's nephew al-Malik al-Adil (1200-18). It has twelve towers. Inside there is a small Byzantine chapel, two cemeteries, the ruins of a medieval Benedictine monastery, the Franciscan convent, and a magnificent basilica built by Spanish Franciscans in 1924. The views are breath-taking, and enhanced by the beauty of the basilica.

*Nain.* After coming down to the main road a further 5 miles (8 km.) on is the village of Nain, where a Franciscan chapel was built in 1880 on the site of the ancient sanctuary, commemorating the healing of the widow's son.

*Jenin.* Passing through Afula (5 miles, 8 km.) Jenin is reached after 11¼ miles (18 km.). According to tradition it was here that Jesus cured the ten lepers, of whom only one, a Samaritan, rendered thanks (Luke 17.11-19). There was bitter hatred between Jews and Samaritans, and it is only in a border town such as this that a mixed group, even of lepers, could have lived.

*Sebaste (Sebastiyyah).* 22 miles (35 km.) further on a turn-off on the left leads to Sebaste, the ancient Samaria, capital of Israel. The remains of a fine basilica in honour of St. John the Baptist, built by the Crusaders in 1165 on the ruins of a Byzantine basilica, can be seen amid the ruins of the town, that are largely of the Roman period. It is sparsely inhabited by a few Christians. 7½ miles (12 km.) further on is the town of Nablus, (pop. c.44,000), almost wholly Muslim. A winding road to the right leads up to the ancient Shechem (Shekhem) where in the fifth to fourth century BC the Samaritans built their Temple, and where they still celebrate their Passover. The ruined castle was built by Justinian in 533. Nearby is an octagonal Byzantine church, whose dimensions are closely related to those of the Church of the House of Peter (above, pp.49-50) at Capharnaum and to those of the Dome of the Rock (below, p.75). While in the two latter cases the object was to enclose and display a sacred room and a sacred rock, it is not clear what the object was here.

*Jacob's Well.* On the eastern outskirts of Nablus the well is venerated where Jesus met the Samaritan woman (John 4.7-29), who recognized him as the Messiah. C.380 a cruciform church was built here, incorporating an earlier baptistery. It was destroyed in the Samaritan revolt of 529, and again by the Arabs. The Crusaders built a new church there. The reconstruction of 1914 is still incomplete. The well is 75 ft. (23 m.) deep. From here to Jerusalem it is 39 miles (63 km.). The road passes through Bira, where Jesus' parents are said to have sought him sorrowing after he had stayed behind disputing with the doctors in the Temple when he was twelve years old (Luke 2.42).

After a visit to Jerusalem (John 7.10ff.; see below p.74), where he taught in the Temple, Jesus escaped arrest and went away across the Jordan to where John had baptized (above, p.42). There he learnt of Lazarus' illness and death, and went to Bethany (John 11.1-44), where he raised Lazarus from the dead. The village is known today in Arabic as al-Azariyyah, the L of Lazarus having been absorbed by the Arabic definite article *al-*. There was already a church here by 390. Following an earthquake, it was rebuilt in the fifth century, and enlarged because of the number of pilgrims visiting the tomb of Lazarus. A new church was built over the tomb by the Crusaders, and a Benedictine house was founded beside it in 1138. The whole was in ruins by the end of the fourteenth century. The present Franciscan church and convent was built over part of the ruins in 1954, and the adjacent Greek Orthodox Church in 1965. The tomb of Lazarus itself is entered by a precipitous staircase from the street between the two churches, and is under the care of the Department of Antiquities and Ancient Monuments. Up the street is a cross-roads. The road on the right leads to Bethphage.

*Bethphage.* There are frequent buses from Jerusalem to the Mount of Olives and Bethany. Bethphage lies up a track.

It was from Bethphage that according to the Gospels Jesus made his

triumphant entry into Jerusalem on the first Palm Sunday (Matt.21.
1-2), after a short stay at both Ephraim (a village some 12½ miles (20
km.) north of Jerusalem, the present al-Tayyibah) and also, according
to the synoptists, at Jericho, where a blind man was healed (Mark
10.46). Here too the tax-collector Zacchaeus had climbed a sycamore to
get a glimpse of Jesus, and had been rewarded by a visit to his house
(Luke 19.1-10). The ruins of the ancient Jericho, a huge *tel*, lie outside
the modern settlement.

The road up from Jericho is called in Arabic *tal'at al-damm*, the
ascent of blood, in Hebrew *ma'aleh adummim*, and passes by the Inn of
the Good Samaritan (above, p.41). The road winds in through
Bethany, but Bethphage lies away from the present main road high up
on the right. The Roman road travelled more directly. At present the
name Bethphage is attached to the church and convent of the
Franciscans lying in a hollow below, built on medieval ruins in 1883.
There are beautiful medieval paintings on stone, one recording Jesus'
meeting with Lazarus' sisters (John 11.20-30). It was in this vicinity
that Jesus sent the disciples into the village to fetch him an ass (Mark
11.1-2) and it is from this church that the Palm Sunday Procession, led
by the Latin Patriarch, starts.

11.   Qumran, site of discovery of Dead Sea Scrolls

12. The Dome of the Rock, Jerusalem

13. Aqsa Mosque, fountain ot el-Kas

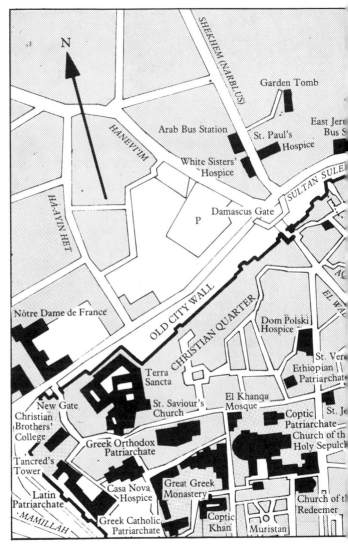

N

SHEKHEM (NABLUS)

Garden Tomb

East Jer
Bus S

HANEVI'IM

Arab Bus Station

St. Paul's
Hospice

White Sisters'
Hospice

SULTAN SULE

HA-AYIN HET

P

Damascus Gate

AQ

Nôtre Dame de France

OLD CITY WALL

CHRISTIAN QUARTER

Dom Polski
Hospice

EL WA

St. Ver

Terra
Sancta

Ethiopian
Patriarchate

New Gate

St. Saviour's
Church

El Khanqa
Mosque

Christian
Brothers'
College

Coptic
Patriarchate

St. J

Greek Orthodox
Patriarchate

Church of th
Holy Sepulch

Tancred's
Tower

Casa Nova
Hospice

Great Greek
Monastery

Latin
Patriarchate

Church of t
Redeemer

MAMILLAH

Coptic
Khan

Muristan

Greek Catholic
Patriarchate

12. The Old City

SALAH ED DIN

IBN SINA

HARUN ER-RASHID

Rockefeller
Museum

ah's
o

Post Office

Stork Tower

YERIHO
(YERICHO)

Herod's Gate

MUSLIM QUARTER

Muslim
Cemetery

EL MATHANA

Indian
Hospice

QADISIEH

Pools of
Bethsaida

on's
es
ah's Cave

Church of St. Anne

Convent of
the Sisters
of Sion

St. Anne's
Seminary

RAYA
ustrian
Iospice

Monastery of the
Flagellation

SHA'AR HA'ARAYOT

Lion Gate (or
St. Stephen's
Gate)

Church of
Our Lady of
the Spasm

El Umariyeh
School

Birket Israel

Bab el-Asbat

Bab Hitta

Bab el-Atim

Bab el-
Ghawanima

Solomon's Dome

Bab en Nazir

Solomon's
Throne

Golden Gate

Muslim
Orphanage

Bab el-Hadid

Dome of the Rock

Bab el-Qattanin

Dome of the Chain

HA – OFEL

Bab es Silsila

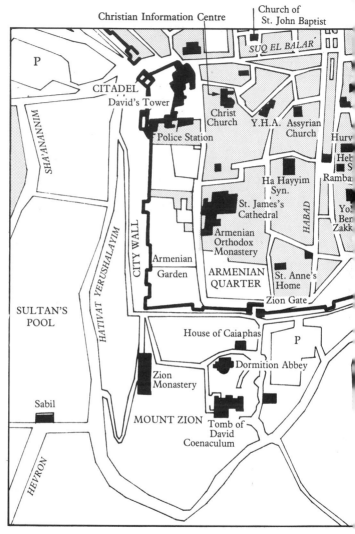

**12. The Old City**

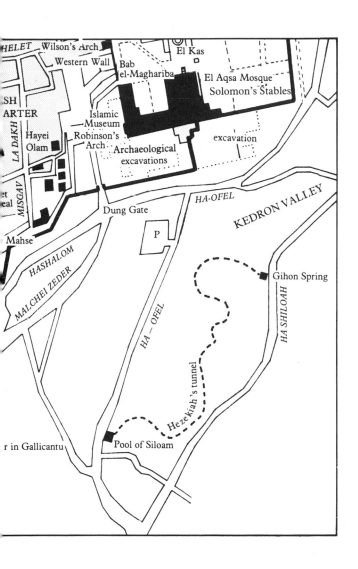

## *Jerusalem, the Holy City*

### *History of the City and its Walls* (see map 12)

As the visitor approaches the Old City of Jerusalem, the splendid walls built in 1535-8 by the Ottoman Sultan Sulayman the Magnificent stretch out proudly before him. They convey an illusion of immemorial antiquity. The Old City has formed the present shape since AD 135 only; Sulayman's walls follow those laid out for the Emperor Hadrian's Aelia Capitolina. Part of his Roman northern gate has recently been exposed beneath Sulayman's Damascus Gate. Innumerable pilgrims and tourists have been perplexed by the fact that Golgotha and the Holy Sepulchre now lie within the city walls, and some explanation of the various changes is necessary. The different stages were finally ascertained in the 1960s by Dame Kathleen Kenyon, of the British School of Archaeology in Jerusalem, by the most rigorous archaeological methods. Subsequent discoveries have confirmed the validity of her findings. The original city, of the Jebusites and of David, lay outside these walls to the south-east.

The present Old City, one quarter of a square mile in area, is built on two ridges some 2700 ft (830 m.) above sea level. They are traversed by the valley Flavius Josephus called the Tyropoeon, which is partly filled in by the debris of 3,000 years of occupation. Some idea of the depth of this fill can be gained from outside the Damascus Gate, although it has only been cleared down to the level of AD 135. On the east the city is bounded by the Silwan, or Siloam, valley, that of the ancient brook Kedron, and on the west and south by the Valley of Hinnom, or Gehenna. The Hinnom, the Tyropoeon and the Kedron merge south of the Ophel Hill, selected in ancient times because it controlled the spring Gihon, later the Virgin's Fountain, one of Jerusalem's only two permanent sources of water supply. Here, c.996 BC, David's forces crept up the water-shaft (2 Sam.5.8) and took the Jebusite city, and made it the capital of Judah. The whole of this lay on the Ophel Hill, south of the Temple Mount.

This city was built partly on a series of artificial stone terraces; no building remains of David's city, to which he brought the sacred Ark to which Solomon gave a permanent home in the Temple. This area was first enclosed by Solomon, when an enormous terrace was constructed, the *Haram al-Sharif*, the Noble Sanctuary, as it is called in Arabic, which today includes the *Qubbat al-Sakhra*, the Dome of the Rock, the Aqsa Mosque, and a number of auxiliary buildings and offices, enclosing a sixth of the whole area of the Old City, still today the dominant feature of Jerusalem. Solomon's Temple was destroyed when Nebuchadrezzar captured Jerusalem in 586 BC, but rebuilt on the same plan when the exiles returned from Babylon in 538 BC. It was to make the Temple more worthy and glorious that Herod the Great undertook its rebuilding c.20 BC, extending the terrace to its present area of 520 yards (c.480 metres) from north to south, and 325 yards (300 m.) from west to east. This had the effect of burying all preceding structures, which included also Solomon's palace and the palace of Pharaoh's daughter, and other buildings. In the eighth to seventh c.BC the city spilled over westwards as far as what is now the the Armenian Quarter. This was probably outside the walls which have been discovered in the present Jewish Quarter. During this period elaborate water systems were constructed.

After the return from the Babylonian Exile in 538 BC, the population of the city, which had dwindled during the exilic period, greatly increased. The Temple was rebuilt at once, but the walls were not repaired until the governorate of Nehemiah, 445-433 BC. Some of his roughly built, but solid, work still survives. First under Persia, and then under Alexander the Great, Jerusalem was a city of little importance. Under his successors after 198 BC, the Seleucids of Syria, would-be rulers of Jerusalem, took part in the contentions for the Syrian throne. It was this that caused Antiochus Epiphanes to sack and destroy the city, and to profane the Temple in 168 BC. To control it he built the Akra fortress, on a site still disputed, but most probably that of the Citadel.

This may at first have been an isolated building, but shortly, either under Simon Maccabeus (143-135 BC) or John Hyrcanus (135-105 BC), all of the Upper City (the present Armenian and Jewish Quarters), was walled. The next extension of the city, and of its walls, belongs to the rebuilding operations of Herod the Great (37 to 4 BC), whose reign was a grand climacteric in the history of Israel in more ways than one.

An Idumaean, a Romanophil, and opposed to the archaism of Jewish orthodoxy, his aim was to make the city rank in grandeur with other great cities of the Roman Empire. The rebuilding of the Temple is to be seen in this context, not in that of piety. Although not a vestige of his Temple remains, in precise accord with the prediction of Jesus Christ that not one stone would be left upon another (Matt.24.2ff), the stupendous platform of the Haram al-Sharif is still buttressed on the south and east by his retaining walls, or at least always in the lower courses. The huge stones, laid brickwise in headers and stretchers, of which it is constructed, are markedly different from later building, as can be seen clearly. Likewise dominant over the city is the Citadel, of which one tower, known erroneously as the Tower of David, is certainly Herod's work, as are some of the lower courses elsewhere there. However, most of his palace lies either below the present police barracks or to the south of it. North-west of the Temple he built a second fortress, named the Antonia, from which the Temple area could be garrisoned and controlled, approximately on the site of or near the present Omariyeh College. He likewise built a theatre in the Greek fashion, and, like other rulers, made special provision for water conservation. Among other reservoirs, his Serpents' Pool, Tower Pool, Sheep Pool and the Strouthion (quince) Pool, remain today. The last named lay inside the Antonia Fortress. North of the Temple lay the sheep market, and to the west other markets and storehouses astride the Tyropoeon Valley. This was now included within a second wall, which stopped short on the western side, immediately east of the little hill of Golgotha. Here, in the area covered now by the Holy Sepulchre and the adjoining properties, was a quarry, outside the city wall. Archaeologically it is certain that this area was unoccupied between the seventh century BC and AD 135, when the Roman city of Aelia Capitolina was laid out by the Emperor Hadrian with the intention of obliterating all trace of the earlier Jerusalem. It is clear that the sites of

1. Dome of the Rock. 2. Dome of the Chain. 3. Dome of the Ascension. 4. Summer Pulpit. 5. El-Kas Fountain. 6. The Mosque of Al-Aqsa. 7. Solomon's stables. 8. Golden Gate. 9. Solomon's Throne. 10. Gate of the Tribes (Bab el Asbat). 11. (Bab Hitta). 12. Gate of Gloom (Bab el-Atim). 13. Antonia Fortress remains. 14. Bab el-Ghawanima. 15. Bab el-Nazir. 16. (Bab el-Haded). 17. Cotton Merchants' Gate (Bab el-Qattanin). 18. Bab el-Matara. 19. Chain Gate (Bab el-Silsila). 20. Bab el-Mughariba. 21. Islamic Museum. 22. Sabil Qait Bey. 23. The Stairs of Scales of Souls. 24. Dome of Suleiman Pasha. 25. Sabil. 26. Sabil of Sheikh Budir. 27. Bab Sitti Mariam or St. Stephen's Gate (Lion Gate). 28. Single Gate (filled). 29. Triple Gate (filled). 30. Double Gate (filled). 31. Robinson's Arch. 32. The Western (Wailing) Wall. 33. Small Western Wall. 34. Suq el-Qattanin. 35. Wilson's Arch. 36. Omariyyeh School. 37. Condemnation Chapel. 38. Sisters of Sion Convent. 39. Church of St. Anne. 40. Muslim Tombs. 41. Muslim Cemetery.

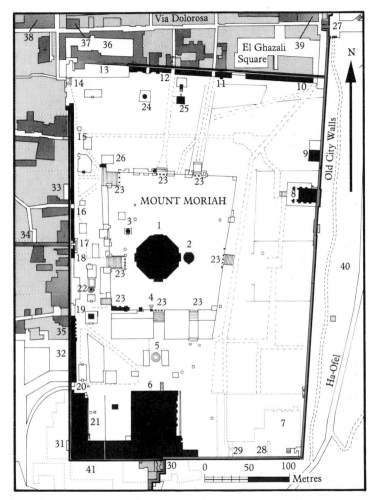

Via Dolorosa

El Ghazali
Square

N

MOUNT MORIAH

Old City Walls

Ha-Ofel

0    50    100

Metres

13. The Haram al-Sharif

Golgotha and the Holy Sepulchre *can* be authentic. It does not prove, of course, that they *are* authentic. But, among many other good reasons, it can be said that when the Empress Helena came to build the Church of the Holy Sepulchre c.326 the site was *within* the Roman city, and that this must have been as perplexing to her as it has been to later pilgrims and tourists. The tradition held by the Church of Jerusalem that this was the veritable site must have seemed to her to be of great strength for her to be persuaded to build on this site.

After the death of Herod the Great in 4 BC, foreign Procurators ruled until AD 40, when Herod Agrippa, Herod the Great's grandson, was allowed by Rome to rule over much of his grandfather's kingdom. Herod Agrippa died in AD 44. These four years were ones of hectic building activity: David's Jerusalem covered 10·87 acres, Herod the Great's 140 acres, and now Herod Agrippa increased it to 310 acres. A new wall encompassed the southern end of the western ridge, then ran east until it met the Kedron Valley, and then north again until it met the Temple terrace. On the north side a wall lying farther north than in the time of Herod the Great was built upon the line of the present north wall of the Old City, and linked with the earlier western and eastern walls. It was in this way that the quarry area of the Holy Sepulchre and Golgotha came to be surrounded by the walls. Part of this wall is visible below the Roman remains at the Damascus Gate, and there is clear evidence to connect it with the reign of Herod Agrippa.

Twenty-two years later the cruelty and misrule of successive procurators culminated in provoking open rebellion. Warfare began in AD 66. First Galilee, and then Judaea, was subdued by the future Emperor Vespasian. Soon after he had been proclaimed Emperor in AD 69 he left for Rome. In AD 70 it fell to his son Titus to reduce Jerusalem by a siege that lasted from the spring until the autumn. Titus's Arch in Rome records the capture of the city. Sacred objects from the Temple are carried in the procession. Leading Jews are shown as prisoners. The city is shown as a desolation. Literary evidence witnesses that the walls were destroyed and that the Temple was burnt. Only three towers of Herod's palace on the Citadel site remained, and part of the southern wall, where Titus left a garrison. The Xth Legion Fretensis ruled over a ruin. Shortly some 800 veterans were brought in to repopulate the city. Elsewhere there were several risings in centres of Jewish settlement, and in 129, Hadrian had visited Jerusalem. What prompted him to

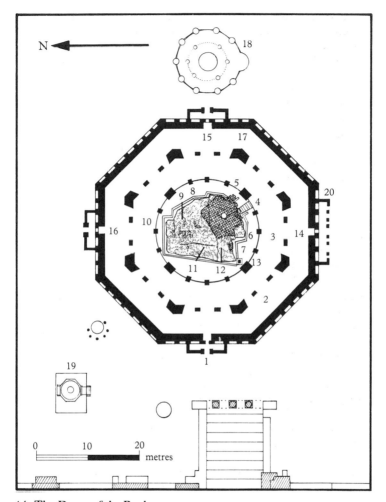

## 14. The Dome of the Rock

1. Western gate (entrance). 2. 1st arcade. 3. 2nd arcade. 4. Steps to the 'Well of Souls'.
5. Place of Prayer of Solomon. 6. Place of Prayer of David. 7. Place of Prayer of Absalom.
8. Place of Prayer of Elijah. 9. Chipped Surface in Sacred Rock. 10. Wooden Balustrade.
11. Transverse Crack (earthquake of 1067). 12. 'Muhammad's Footprint'. 13. Turret
Cupboard (Hairs from Muhammad's Beard). 14. Southern Gate (Mecca). 15. Judgement
Gate. 16. Paradise Gate. 17. Inscription (Caliph al-Mansur). 18. Dome of the Chain.
19. Dome of the Ascension. 20. The Magpie stone.

determine to rebuild Jerusalem as a Roman city is not clear. Its inauguration with solemn pagan rites and a furrow ploughed ceremonially to demarcate the walls was the immediate provocation of Bar Kochba's revolt (AD 132-5). It was only after it had been suppressed that Hadrian's plan could go ahead to build Aelia Capitolina: Aelia because his full name was Publius Aelius Hadrianus, Capitolina because the city was dedicated to the triad of Roman deities, Jupiter, Juno and Minerva. Much of the lay-out of this typical Roman city survives in the present grid of streets. The northern wall was approximately the present one, as were those on the west and east, where their limits are controlled by the lines of the high ridges. The south wall followed, for the most part, the line of the present one. Part of the Triumphal Arch built by Hadrian survives as the Ecce Homo Arch, with parts of it within the Convent of the Sisters of Sion. Some of the columns of the main street, the Cardo Maximus, are to be seen in the Russian Convent commonly known as the Russian excavations, near the Church of the Holy Sepulchre (below, p.92).

As said already, Constantine the Great's declaration of Christianity as a licit religion was a turning point in the history of Jerusalem. In 326 he sent his mother, the Empress Helena, thither, and under her supervision the pagan city began to be transformed into what now became the focus – as it had been the epicentre – of the Christian world. First Golgotha and the Holy Sepulchre, then other churches and monasteries, were raised in rapid succession, in the Old City, near Gethsemane, on the Mount of Olives, and in Bethlehem and other sites made sacred by traditional memories. Under the Empress Eudoxia new churches and pilgrim hospices were built; under Justinian (527-65) the city was again enlarged. Then in 636 Jerusalem fell to the Arabs.

The change of ruler made little immediate difference. The Caliph 'Umar carefully avoided praying in the Holy Sepulchre, lest, he said, his followers should make it a mosque. Where he prayed is the adjacent small Mosque of 'Umar close by the courtyard of the Church of the Holy Sepulchre. He cleaned the Temple terrace of dirt and debris, and built a simple mosque at the south end, the origin of the Aqsa Mosque. By 680 it was a large wooden structure capable of accommodating three thousand persons. What was now to give Jerusalem a wholly new character was the construction by the Caliph Abd al-Malik b.Marwan

(685-705) of the Dome of the Rock, built in 687-91 (below, p.74). This, one of the most splendid constructions achieved by mankind, was complemented in 780 by the building of the Aqsa Mosque in stone, but none of this first building survives (below, p.76). It was the end of an era of generally peaceable coexistence when the mad Caliph al-Hakim gave the order for the destruction of the Holy Sepulchre and other Christian buildings in 1009. Then, although there was some reconstruction, the city was subject for the rest of the century to the disturbances and violence brought about by the Seljuq Turks.

On 15 July 1099 the Crusaders took the city by storm from the north, west and south. As in Byzantine times, new churches were built, and the Qubbat al-Sakhra became the *Templum Domini*, The Temple of the Lord. The Citadel, with the adjacent royal palace, once again dominated the city. The southern wall receded to its earlier position, leaving Mount Sion and the former city of David outside. The Crusaders were finally expelled in 1187. Their Ayyubid and Mamluk successors were in general tolerant towards Christians and Jews, but themselves controlled the Holy Sepulchre. Jerusalem had no political importance for them, but Muslim religious learning was encouraged. Commercially there was considerable development. At the end of the fifteenth century the expulsion of the Jews from Spain brought a wave of immigrants whose presence in the city can still be noted. The defences were unimportant, and so neglected. In December 1517 the Ottoman Sultan Selim the Grim took the city, but it was left to his son, Sulayman the Magnificent, to rebuild the walls and gates, and give it the aspect it has today. Nevertheless his successors neglected the city as indeed they neglected much else. By the seventeenth century there were only 10,000 citizens, and by 1800 only 6,000. It was under the British Mandate (effectively 1917-48) and since, first under Jordanian rule (1948-67), and then under the Republic of Israel, that the city has been restored, repopulated and developed.

## (i) *The Temple Area*

From the height of the Mount of Olives a splendid view is unfolded of what Arabs speak of as the Noble Sanctuary, the *Haram al-Sharif*. No city on earth can boast quite so superb a prospect. Its central building, the Dome of the Rock, *Qubbat al-Sakhra*, rises from the vast terrace which itself is like some proud ship at sea. As Jesus rode down on the first Palm Sunday the actual Rock was hidden below the grandiose constructions of Herod, with the terrace surrounded by colonnades on all four sides. Which of the three possible routes from the Mount of Olives he used is not ascertainable. Possibly the steepest, the central one past the back of the Church of *Dominus Flevit*, is the most likely, although the Palm Sunday Procession (re-introduced in 1933) follows an easier route to the south. The Church of *Dominus Flevit*, commemorating Jesus weeping over Jerusalem, was built in 1955, after excavations had disclosed the ruins of a fifth century monastery and a large cemetery. According to tradition, Jesus rode directly to the Temple on the first Palm Sunday, entering through the Golden Gate, but according to Josephus the Golden Gate was used by priests only. Careful reading of Matt.21.10 suggests that he entered the Temple after passing through the city, in which case it would have been more natural if he had entered through St Stephen's Gate (Ar.*Bab Sitti Mariam*, the Gate of My Lady Mary).

Entering the Temple area Jesus would have seen double colonnades on the north, west and east. The eastern colonnade was known as Solomon's Porch. The southern colonnade had 162 pillars set in four rows, 81 feet high. These enclosed the Court of the Gentiles. The Temple itself most likely stood somewhat north of where the Dome of the Rock now stands; the precise position of its components has never been ascertained, and the exact position of the Holy of Holies is not known. The Beautiful Gate, on the east side of the Temple complex, led to the Court of the Women. Stairs, the Nicanor Gate, led from it to the Court of the Men containing the Altar of Burnt Sacrifice on a terrace raised above it. Behind it to the west lay the Temple proper, and within the Holy of Holies. The Altar of Burnt Sacrifice is thought to have been at what is now the centre of the Dome of the Rock, and on it fire burned day and night. The animals were slaughtered on the north side.

Everything [says Josephus] to delight eye and heart was presented by the outward appearance of the temple . . . It dazzled the eye like sunlight. To strangers approaching Jerusalem it shone out from afar like a snow clad hill; for, where it was not golden, it radiated a brilliant white.

The Temple is mentioned on numerous occasions in the Gospels. Here (Luke 1.5-22) the angel Gabriel appeared to Zacharias, heralding

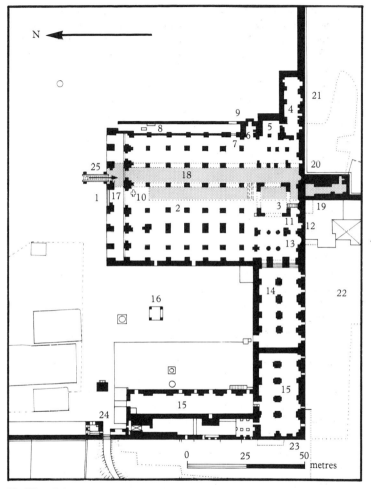

## 15. The al-Aqsa Mosque

1. Main entrance. 2. Nave with six aisles. 3. Saladin's *Mihrab* (prayer niche). 4. Site of Omar's mosque. 5. Forty Martyrs mosque. 6. *Mihrab* of Zacharias. 7. Columns of original structure. 8. Well of the Leaf. 9. Gate of Elijah. 10. Tombs of the Sons of Aaron. 11. Pulpit. 12. *Mihrab* of Moses. 13. *Mihrab* of Jesus. 14. Women's Mosque. 15. Islamic Museum. 16. Dome of Yusuf. 17. Porch. 18. Old Aqsa. 19. El-Zawiye el-Kuntaniye (Crusader structure). 20. Double Gate (filled). 21. Old City Walls. 22. Archaeological Excavations. 23. Robinson's Arch. 24. Maghrabi Gate. 25. Stairs to old entrance to el-Aqsa.

the birth of St John Baptist. Here (Luke 2.22) Mary came for her ritual Purification, for the Presentation of the Child Jesus in the Temple; and here (Luke 2.41) 'his parents went every year to Jerusalem according to the custom of the feast' of the Passover. Jesus' visit at twelve years old was only one such visit (Luke 2.42). It was in Solomon's Porch that Jesus was walking up and down when the Jews tried to draw him into an argument (John 10.23ff.) Here too the earliest Christians met (Acts 3.12-16). Here Jesus attended the Feast of the Tabernacles (John 7.1ff), with its solemn libations of water, and proclaimed 'If any man thirst, let him come to me and drink.' Other scenes, too, took place here, and the Cleansing of the Temple, which John 2.14-16 places at the beginning of Jesus' public activity, occurred for the synoptists on the first Palm Sunday, or the day following (Matt.21.12ff., Mark 11.15-17). Finally, here, as Jesus died, so the veil of the Temple was rent in front of the Holy of Holies (Matt.27.40). Not a single stone of it, he prophesied (Matt.24.2), would remain upon another. It is so today.

After he had taken Jerusalem in AD 70, the Emperor Titus destroyed the Temple and burnt it. In AD 135 the Emperor Hadrian built a temple to Jupiter here. The Emperor Julian the Apostate (361-3) encouraged the Jews to rebuild it, but his successor, Jovian, stopped the work. It was not venerated as a sacred site in Byzantine times, and in 638 the Caliph Omar found it used as a rubbish dump. He erected a wooden mosque here, probably where the Aqsa Mosque now stands.

It was the Caliph 'Abd al-Malik b. Marwan (685-705), when faced by a rival Caliph, Ibn al-Zubayr, at Mecca, who determined to prevent his influence being spread over Syria by pilgrims returning from Mecca, and to substitute the Sakhra, or Rock, for the Kaaba:

this Rock, of which it is reported that upon it the Apostle of God set his foot when he ascended into heaven, shall be unto you in the place of the Kaaba. Then 'Abd al-Malik built above the Rock a dome . . . and the people took the custom of circumambulating the Rock, even as they had paced round the Kaaba.

Another of his aims, it seems, was to prevent the greatness of the Holy Sepulchre and its magnificence dazzling the minds of Muslims. The building he erected (687-91), the earliest surviving Muslim building in existence, and beyond cavil still the most excellent, has a long history of architectural antecedents, in circular temples in Greece and mausoleums derived from them in Rome. Similar arrangements have already been noted in the churches at Capharnaum and on Mount Gerizim, with almost similar dimensions, and the same principles occur in sixth century churches at Ravenna and in Syria. The rotunda of the Church of the Holy Sepulchre has almost identical measurements, and, as excavated by Schick and described by Vincent in the early part of this century, so had the Church of the Ascension (below, p.104) on the Mount of Olives. The Dome of the Rock, however, preserves not only its original ground plan but all its original arches and internal mosaic decorations. Externally the Ottoman Turks substituted faience tiles for mosaics in the sixteenth century, and many of these were replaced in 1963, when the original gilded wooden dome was replaced by the existing one of aluminium alloyed with gold. It is agreeable news that when possible it is intended to remove this, replacing it with gilded wood once again.

Abd al-Malik b. Marwan not only wished to surpass the Holy Sepulchre in magnificence; he also wished to emphasise the superior truth of Islam as opposed to Christianity. Thus above the mosaics is a broad blue band, bearing Kufic inscriptions in gold letters. All of these refer pejoratively to Christ: they are quotations from the Qu'ran. For example:

*Sura xvii.111*: Say – Praise be to God who has had no Son or companion in his government, and who requires no helper to save him from dishonour; praise him.

*Sura lvii.2:* . . . speak the truth only of God. The Messiah Jesus is only the son of Mary, the ambassador of God, and his Word which he deposited in Mary. Believe then in God and his ambassador, and do not maintain that there are three . . . God is one, far be it from him that he should have had a son.

*Sura xix.34:* . . . God is not so constituted that he could have a son; be that far from him.

The mosaics are of different periods, but all, most probably, by Syrian Christian artists. The law of Islam forbade the representation of human and animal forms, but the grapes and ears of corn that occur with great frequency are the work of those accustomed to these devices as emblems of the Last Supper. In the drum the gold cubes are set at an angle tilted forward at 30°, so that they appear brighter than the motifs. The reverse is the case on the inner face of the inner octagon. In this and in the inner circle the columns have all been removed from churches, and some bear their original crosses. The windows all belong to Sulayman the Magnificent's restoration of 1552, and the carved ceilings are Mamluk work of the thirteenth century. The reliquary beside the Rock is believed to contain a hair from the Prophet Muhammad's beard. Below the Rock is a cave known in Arabic as Bir al-Arwah, The Well of Souls. Those Muslims who prayed there in former times were given a certificate, to be buried with them, entitling them to admission to Paradise. The dimensions and plan of the building are given in plan 14.

A great number of buildings are contained within the Haram al-Sharif (see plan 13). On the north side the Bab al-Atim, known today as the Bab al-Malik Faysal, is closed to the public. There are eight entrances on the west side, all of which may be used by visitors; the three on the south side and both of those on the left are kept closed. Many of them display fine Mamluk work. There are four minarets, on the north side, at the north-west corner, near the Gate of the Chain, and at the south-west corner. There are a number of fountains (*sabil*), raised platforms for prayers (*mastaba*), independent *mihrabs* (niches indicating the direction to be assumed in prayer) and *qubba*, small domes of a commemorative nature. Of especial elegance are the Dome of the Chain, perhaps simply a kiosk, the *Qubbat al-Miraj*, commemorating the Prophet Muhammad's mystical ascent into heaven, the principal ablutions fountain known as el-Kas, and, at a lower level on the west side of the Dome of the Rock, the supremely elegant *Sabil* or Fountain of the Egyptian Sultan Qayt-bay, given by him in 1482. It is the only existing example of a carved masonry stone dome outside Cairo. (It is currently (1981) shored up with scaffolding and under repair, but even so its beauty is still apparent.)

At the south end of the terrace is the Aqsa Mosque, so called 'the most distant' shrine, the furthest Abrahamic shrine from the Kaaba at Mecca. After the Caliph Omar's crude mosque (above, p.74) a larger building was constructed 'by setting great beams on some remains of ruins', capable of holding 3,000 men at once. This had been done c.715-6, evidently using the ruins of the Royal Porch. This was destroyed by an earthquake. Its successor was similarly damaged in 1033, and rebuilt in 1035, by the Fatimid Caliph al-Zahir. This gave the mosque its final form, with six aisles, the central nave being double the width of the side aisles, with a wooden dome in front of the *mihrab*. The plan was almost that of al-Mahdi in 780, and one still enters through his doorway. About one third of the mosque had to be rebuilt

14.   Dormition Abbey, Jerusalem

15.   The Church of All Nations, Gethsemane

The Beauty of Jerusalem

in 1938-42. Then in 1969 it was badly damaged by fire that had been deliberately started in three places, which destroyed much of the marble panelling, some of the mosaics, and the superb pulpit, inlaid with ivory and mother-of-pearl, which was the gift of Saladin in 1168. The repairs to the mosaics, some of which have had to be completely reconstructed, are the work of an artist first employed in the mosque in 1927. Behind the pulpit is a stone taken from the Church of the Ascension (below, p.104), alleged to bear the footprint of the ascending Christ. To its right a pair of columns close together are said not to permit persons to pass through who have not been born in lawful wedlock. Beyond, to the right, is a long building with eight bays, known as the Mosque of the Women. It is in current use as a repair workshop. To the left of the *mihrab* is another pair of columns similar to those just mentioned, and then a small mosque, known as the Mosque of Omar, with an interesting *mihrab*. Just north of it is a small oratory known as the Mosque of the Forty Witnesses, and, behind it, another oratory known as the Place of Zacharias. In Crusader times the building was used as a church by the Knights Templar, and this gave rise to a myth, wholly without foundation, that the mosque was originally built as a church. Plan 15 displays the dimensions and lay-out of the existing building. Near the main entrance the graves of St Thomas Becket's murderers are pointed out.

In the courtyard on the extreme south-west a large building, former-ly known as the Mosque of the Moors, contains the Islamic Museum, a magpie collection of objects presented to the Aqsa and to the Dome of the Rock from time to time, together with woodwork and sculpture re-moved from them in the course of necessary repairs. There is a note-worthy collection of Qu'rans of different periods. The elegant metal screen, which the Crusaders placed round the *Sakhra* in the Dome of the Rock, is exhibited behind a table where two guardians sit. There are fine views from the southern windows. Near the entrance a very elegant mosque lamp of the Mamluk period has a case to itself, near a case of porcelain and twentieth century English china. There is no catalogue or guide available, but one is said to be in preparation.

*

To gain some impression of the Temple area in the time of Jesus a visit should be made to the Holyland Hôtel, where a scale model of the

Temple and the city as reconstructed by Herod is displayed. It is on the scale 1:50, and prepared from details supplied by the distinguished archaeologist Professor Michael Avi-Yonah.

## (ii) The Last Supper and Mount Sion

As noted above (p.64), the Sion which was the city of David was on the eastern ridge of the Holy City; but the wrong ascription to the southern end of the western ridge made in medieval times still persists. No buses reach this area, but coaches gain access to it by taking a circuitous route outside the walls. It is reached easily on foot from the Jaffa Gate, turning right to the south past the Citadel and through the Armenian Quarter (below, p.106), and leaving the walled city through the Sion Gate, otherwise known as the Bab Nabi Daud, or the Jewish Quarter Gate.

*The Citadel* as it stands is largely Mamluk work of the fourteenth century AD. Traditionally the tall tower at the entrance is known as King David's Tower, but it was in fact constructed by Herod the Great, as its huge courses of masonry display. It formed part of a large palace complex built by him, extending beyond the present Citadel into the Armenian Quarter, re-using fortifications of the Maccabaean period (above, p.14). This was the principal seat of government in Jerusalem under the Maccabees, the Romans, the Byzantines, the Arabs, the Crusaders, Saladin and the Turks. In the view of some authorities it was the *Praetorium* in which Pilate tried Jesus (John 18.28-19.16) (but see below, p.87). Just beyond it to the south is the Police Barracks, after which the Armenian Quarter begins. From it to the complex of buildings on Mount Sion is about 650 yards (600 m.).

Passing through the walls at the Sion Gate, on the right up a lane is the site of the House of Caiaphas as claimed by the Armenians (below, p.110). A little further on is the Basilica of the Dormition, the traditional site of the Falling Asleep of Our Lady. The present church and buildings were erected in 1898-1910. The crypt contains a recumbent statue of Our Lady of great beauty, and, amongst others, an altar, presented by President Houphouët-Boigny of the Ivory Coast, in ivory and ebony, of distinguished elegance. It is on the site of a Church of Our Lady of Mount Sion built by the Crusaders, and demolished by the Arabs in 1219.

Returning back down the lane in order to turn right, there is an iron door, frequently locked, which gives access to a charming garden, in which there is the small Franciscan Church of the Coenaculum (the place of the Last Supper), built in 1936, with very modern decorations. The altar backs on to a medieval building to which access is gained farther down the lane on the left. This contains the Tomb of David, venerated alike by Jews and Muslims, but there is no record of it earlier than the twelfth century AD. Reached by an outside staircase and across a small room is the *Coenaculum*. The tradition is not recorded before the fifth century AD, when it was associated with the already existing tradition attested by 348, that it was here in an 'upper room' that the Holy Spirit descended on the apostles (Acts 1.13, 2.1). However this may be, the only competing site is the Syrian Orthodox Church of St. Mark (below, p. 110), which claims to possess the 'Upper Room', but is sustained only by oral tradition. For this reason the tradition held by the Franciscans, and attested since the fourth century, may seem to be the more plausible. The actual room is divided into two naves by two pillars holding up a vaulted roof of the Crusader period. The elaborate *mihrab*, of superficially Mamluk period, was in fact inserted in 1928 only. To its left a small staircase leads to another small room, of which the door is kept locked. Tradition asserts that the small room is the place of the Descent of the Holy Spirit and the larger the place of the Last Supper. For these reasons, and for the other events that would have taken place here; the institution of the priesthood, the prayer that all may be one, the giving of the new commandment to love one another, the Washing of the Feet, the appearance of Jesus on Easter Day and the institution of the sacrament of Penance, it is spoken of as the 'Mother of Churches'.

Another church on the eastern slope of the ridge, reached across the main road and then by a steep lane, is the Church of St Peter *in Gallicantu* (at the Cockcrow). This is claimed by the Assumptionist Fathers to be the site of the Palace of the High Priest Caiaphas (Mark 14.53ff.). Here Jesus was questioned by him, and here, it is asserted, Peter three times denied his Master. The church is built over excavations by the Assumptionists begun in 1887, before the age of modern scientific archaeology. Traces have been found of a monastic church of the seventh century, together with structures of the Herodian period, including cellars, stables and cisterns. One of these is claimed to be the dungeon in which Jesus spent the night before his crucifixion. The

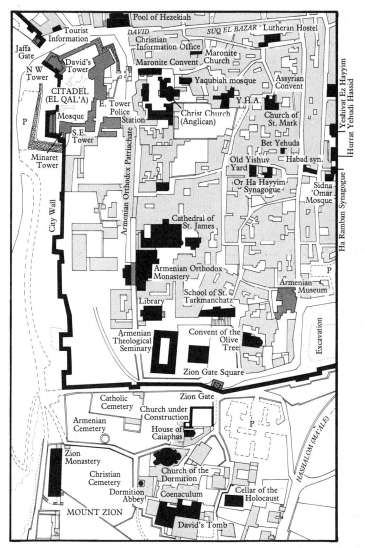

16. The Armenian Quarter and Mount Sion

occupational evidence before the seventh century seems to be wholly domestic, and not to demonstrate any connection with Caiaphas, for whom another house is predicated higher up the hill (below, p.110).

There is a splendid view from the church across the Hinnom (Gehenna) Valley. Below is the Monastery of St. Onuphrius, an Egyptian hermit, whose beard was so luxuriant that it served as his only garment. From the fourth century the burial ground at the bottom has been associated with the Aceldama, the Field of Blood of the Gospel (Matt.27.7-10), bought by the priests with Judas's thirty pieces of silver, or where he hanged himself (Acts 1.18-19).

## (iii) Gethsemane

After celebrating the Last Supper, Jesus went with his disciples across the Kedron Valley to the foot of the Mount of Olives, where there was a garden called Gethsemane (Mark 14.26, 32 and other refs.). It was a place where they went often, for Judas (John 18.2) knew it. Jesus had anticipated Judas's betrayal (Mark 14.17-21), and could quite easily have escaped up the Mount of Olives and beyond into the desert, where innumerable caves could have afforded him concealment. Here, therefore, he stopped to decide whether to stand and face his accusers or to run away.

The Church of All Nations, built in 1924, encloses a rock in the garden in which Jesus prayed. No one can be certain of the exact spot where he prayed, but this one is for certain very close to the well-worn route up to the top of the Mount of Olives before the construction of modern roads. The church replaces two earlier ones, one built between 379 and 384, which was destroyed by an earthquake in c.744-5. A Crusader church was built here c.1170 on a slightly different axis, and preserving some of the mosaic floor of the earlier church, still visible through glass panels in the present floor. This church was abandoned in 1345. The present church is richly decorated with mosaics of high excellence, and the dark glass of the windows throws a sombre light which reflects the idea of Jesus' agony. Outside in the garden are eight ancient olive trees, of which two may possibly be contemporary with him, the others being offshoots of earlier trees. The principal doors of the church on the west side are not in common use, and entry is effected from a door up the lane on the north side of the church. This leads to a

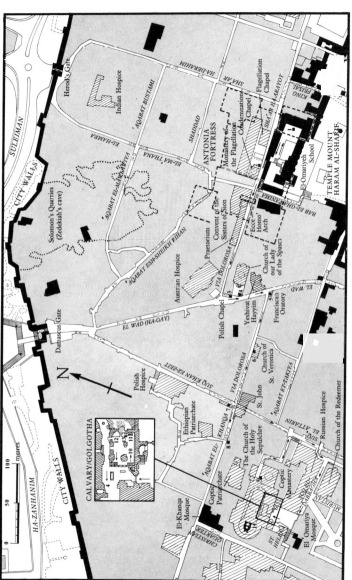

17. The Via Dolorosa

walk along the side of the garden, which itself, while wholly visible, is not accessible to visitors. The word Gethsemane is a Greek form derived from Hebrew *gat shemanim*, oil press, or oil stores.

Leaving by the same door by which one entered, on the opposite side of the lane an ornamental iron-work door enables a view of another garden, which is not accessible to the public. This side of the garden abuts on the Grotto of Gethsemane, which is visible on the far side. The Franciscans have placed an open-air altar here for the use of Anglicans, as an ecumenical gesture.

Returning down the lane, and turning right, very shortly a broad flight of steps leads down to the Church of the Tomb of the Blessed Virgin. Immediately to the right a narrow passage leads to the Grotto of Gethsemane, a cave in which the disciples are believed to have remained asleep whilst Jesus prayed in his Agony. Here Jesus is believed to have been betrayed by Judas Iscariot, and arrested. The Franciscans acquired the grotto in 1392; in the twelfth century it had been adorned with paintings and mosaics, all of which are now almost completely effaced. At the back there is a Jewish tomb of an early period. Except for the three modern altars and a small amount of unobtrusive furnishing, the cave is no doubt much as it has been for many centuries, and perhaps much as it was when the disciples awaited Jesus. The altar on the right hand side was given by Fr Eugene Hoade, OFM, and by his friends. He was a priest who, over a very long period, gave himself to making the Holy Places intelligible to pilgrims. It is convenient to digress here to visit the Church of the Tomb of the Blessed Virgin. That she was assumed into heaven was proclaimed as a doctrine of the Church by Pius XII on 1 November 1950, but the belief was far older, and the Feast of the Assumption on 15 August was made a public holiday in England by King Alfred the Great. He believed that she is as we may hope to be.

An octagonal church already existed here in the time of the Patriarch Juvenal (422-58). Geoffrey de Bouillon built an Abbey here, of St Mary in the Valley of Jehoshaphat, for the Benedictines of Cluny, and in 1130 later Crusaders rebuilt the church in its present form. Later in the century the abbey and its church were destroyed by the Arabs, but the lower church was allowed to remain because of their veneration for Our Lady, as taught in the Qu'ran. The Franciscans obtained it in the fourteenth century, but were expelled in 1757. Since then the Greeks have been in possession with the Armenians. Not only do Abyssinians,

17. Altar of the Nailing to the Cross, Calvary

16. Via Dolorosa

Copts and Syrians enjoy minor rights in the church: even Muslims have a special place for their prayers. Because of the expulsion, the Latins hold no services here.

A square atrium is in front of the church, with steps leading up to a door set in a Crusader arch. On the right, in a chapel dedicated to Sts Anne and Joachim, parents of Our Lady, is the tomb of Queen Mélisande, daughter of Baldwin II and wife of Fulk of Anjou, Kings of Jerusalem. Her Breviary is to be seen in the British Museum. Slightly farther down on the left is the chapel of St. Joseph. Here Mary, wife of King Baldwin III, Constance, mother of Bohémund III, and Matilda, wife of Eric the Good, are buried. At the foot of the steps is a stall for the sale of candles.

One enters what is a perfectly regular cruciform church, with apses at either end to the right and the left. There is a cistern in the left hand apse. Across the crossing a locked door leads to a corridor which gives access to some tombs. On the right a small edicule (Latin *aedicula*, small building) contains the tomb chamber where Our Lady was laid. It has two entrances. An altar slab has been placed over the slab where the body would have lain, and is protected by thick glass. On the right of the edicule is a *mihrab*, indicating the direction of Mecca, where Muslims come to pray from time to time.

## (iv) The Trial and the Via Dolorosa

After Jesus' arrest, he was taken first before the High Priest Caiaphas (above, p.79; below, p.110) and then before the High Priest Annas (below, p.109). The site of the dwelling of the first named is disputed, while that of the second is lost below an Armenian church (below, p.109). Thereafter, early in the morning he appeared before the Sanhedrim, possibly in a court-room in the Temple, of which the location is not known. It was only after that that he was taken before Pilate.

The normal residence of the Roman procurators was the Citadel. A secondary palace had been built by Herod overlooking the Temple Area, known as the Antonia, in honour of Mark Antony. This, like the Citadel, was garrisoned in case of riot on great festivals. On its site a Muslim school, the Omariyyeh College, has succeeded what once was a Turkish barracks. It is set on a rocky platform that rises sharply above the level of the Via Dolorosa, and its tactical significance can at once be appreciated if one goes up the stairs in the middle of the terrace. There a loggia with a window presents a view of the Haram al-Sharif and the whole Temple area with a suddenness which is breath-taking after the narrow street and mean courtyard. Controversy has long raged between these two sites as the place where Pilate gave judgement; the Stations of the Cross, which are conducted each Friday afternoon at 3 p.m. by the Franciscans with touching simplicity and absence of ceremony, start within the Omariyyeh College. The Gospels, except in using the word *Praetorium*, are not specific in locating it precisely. For Philo of Alexandria (d. AD 40), who never refers in any of his works to the existence of Jesus Christ, Pilate normally resided at the Citadel when he came up to Jerusalem from his ordinary residence at Caesarea for the great Jewish festivals. Josephus, equally impartial, says of one of Pilate's successors:

Florus lodged at the palace. On the next day he had a dais placed in front of the building and took his seat. The chief priests, the notables, and the most eminent citizens then presented themselves before the tribunal.

It is precisely such a scene as this that is described in the Gospels.

The Franciscan convent of the Flagellation is on the north side of the Via Dolorosa. In the courtyard on the right is the Chapel of the Scourging; a second chapel on the left commemorates the Condemnation to Death. Here there begins a massive pavement of stone slabs that extends westwards under the Convent of Our Lady of Sion and beyond to under the Greek Orthodox convent with the Greek words above the entrance *tò praitórion* – The Praetorium. It is claimed that this pavement is the Pavement called *Lithostrotos*, and in Hebrew *Gabbatha*, and that it was an integral part of the Antonia Fortress. Across the street stretches the *Ecce Homo* Arch, where Pilate is claimed to have brought Jesus before the people, exclaiming: Behold the man! A further part of this arch is visible in the chapel of the Sisters of Our Lady of Sion; the other side has been destroyed. This is certainly unhistorical: it is a triple arched gate which most likely was built when Hadrian had Aelia Capitolina laid out in 135. The walls here were protected by a ditch and what may have been an ancient cistern, which certainly was still open in June AD 70 because the Romans had to build a ramp across it. The great stone pavement would therefore appear to be later, most probably when the Emperor

Hadrian replanned the city in AD 135, and built a forum here. This may well be the pavement of the forum.

The devotion known as the Way, or Stations, of the Cross has undergone a long development. In Byzantine times pilgrims went in procession from Gethsemane to Calvary, but without stopping on the way. By the eighth century the procession went round the city to the House of Caiaphas on Mount Sion, then to a Praetorium said to be that of Pilate somewhere near the Temple, and finally to Calvary. The present route began to evolve only in the thirteenth century, under Franciscan encouragement. Even then there were different views about the correct route, and only eight stations were observed in Jerusalem. The existing route was finalized only in the eighteenth century, but Stations I, IV, V and VIII were not localized on their present sites until the nineteenth century. The Way of the Cross is thus to be seen for the most part rather with the eye of faith than scrutinized with the scalpel of history. The present Stations, with their locations, are as follows.

*First Station: Jesus is condemned to Death.* As said, the first Station is commemorated in the Omariyyeh College, a former Turkish barracks. The small Franciscan Chapel of the Flagellation is on the right hand side of the convent of that name across the street, on the site of a medieval chapel. Across the courtyard is the Flagellation Museum, which has recently been re-arranged. The work is not yet complete, and a new catalogue is in preparation. The present chapel was built in 1927-9. On the left hand side from the entrance is the Chapel of the Condemnation, restored in 1903-4, and used at one time as a mosque. The floor of this chapel is part of the great pavement already mentioned. Its striations are thought to have been intended to prevent horses slipping. There are also graffiti of Roman soldiers' barrack-room games.

*Second Station: Jesus receives his Cross.* This is commemorated in the street outside the Convent of the Sisters of Our Lady of Sion, whose chapel is known as the Basilica of *Ecce Homo*. This lies down a passage to the left of the entrance; the pavement is striated as before. To the right a staircase leads to the Lithostrotos and to the cistern referred to above. An eighth century tradition has it that the Scala Santa, the Holy Stairs, in Rome were removed from here and taken to Rome by the Empress Helena. Several of the flags have barrack-room graffiti of games similar to hopscotch, mazes, and the game known as Basilicus played with knuckle bones, known to have been popular in the Roman army. The burlesque king was loaded with absurd honours, and put to death at the end of the farce, in a manner which recalls the mockery of Jesus. Farther down the street on the left is the Greek Orthodox convent already mentioned, where a staircase is exhibited as that of the Praetorium. It has also been claimed as the Prison of Christ, but today as that of the Prison of Barabbas.

*Third Station: Jesus falls under his Cross for the first time.* A small chapel, restored in 1947-8, marks the third Station outside the entrance to the former baths of the Hammam al-Sultan. The event is not mentioned in the Gospels.

*Fourth Station: Jesus meets his afflicted Mother.* This is made outside the Armenian Catholic Church of Our Lady of the Spasm. In the crypt, at ancient street level is a large mosaic, belonging probably to the Byzantine Church of St. Sophia (Holy Wisdom).

*Fifth Station: Simon of Cyrene helps Jesus carry his Cross.* The route now begins to lead uphill to Calvary. The street is known in Arabic as Tariq al-Alam, the Street of Sorrows. The oratory here was built in 1895, but the Franciscans had their first convent in Jerusalem here in c.1229-44.

*Sixth Station: Veronica wipes the face of Jesus.* Eighty yards (73 m.) farther on a column inserted in the walls on the left marks the place where a Jerusalem lady, Veronica, wiped Jesus' face with a handkerchief and the imprint of his face is said to have been left upon it. The incident is not mentioned in the Gospels. There is a Greek Catholic (Melkite) chapel here, and the visible ancient remains are probably of a monastery of Saints Cosmas and Damian, built in 548-63. On the opposite side of the street is the Benevolent Arts Workshop, where exquisite needlework is done, making vestments, and supporting 135 poor Arab Christian families, most of the work being done in their homes. It is known as the Veronica Friendship.

*Seventh Station: Jesus falls the second time.* Again, the event is not mentioned in the Gospels. There are two Franciscan chapels here, one above the other. The lower chapel contains a red monolith where a street from east to west crossed the *Cardo Maximus*, or main street, as built by Hadrian in AD 135, running from north to south. Here earlier there had been an old gate, and here probably Jesus left the city for Golgotha.

*Eighth Station: Jesus speaks to the women of Jerusalem.* This Station is marked by a Latin Cross round which are arranged the Greek letters IC XP NI/KA – representing Jesus Christ conquers – in the wall of the Greek church, where the altar on the right commemorates the Eighth Station. Following this Station it is necessary to retrace one's steps to the Seventh Station, and then to turn right, and continue along the Suq Khan al-Zayt (The Bazaar of the Olive Inn), known to the Crusaders as Malcuisinat, or Bad Cookery Street. On the right is a stone staircase, with, at the top, a winding street leading to the Coptic Patriarchal Cathedral of St Anthony, and adjacent the Coptic Chapel of St Helena. At the doorway, of the Crusader period, the shaft of a column marks the Ninth Station. On the left, as one faces the doorway, another doorway leads to a terrace, with, in its centre, the cupola of the Chapel of St Helena in the Church of the Holy Sepulchre (below p.93). On this terrace are very small cells inhabited by Ethiopian monks. They have two small chapels, the lower one reached by a staircase from the upper. They are fastidiously clean, and elegantly decorated in the Ethiopian manner. From the lower chapel a staircase leads down to a door which gives direct access to the courtyard of the Holy Sepulchre.

*Tenth to Fourteenth Stations.* All these are commemorated inside the Church of the Holy Sepulchre, and are described in the next section, VI.v. To reach the Holy Sepulchre one returns along the winding lane to the stone staircase down to the Suq Khan al-Zayt, continuing along it. This is the route taken by the Friday Procession, not through the Ethiopian chapels. The locations of these Stations are unintelligible without some knowledge of the history and development of the Church of the Holy Sepulchre. Their positions within it are:

*Tenth Station: Jesus is stripped of his garments.* In the right hand nave on Calvary.

---

1. Quadrangle. 2. Monastery of Abraham. 3. Armenian Chapel of St James. 4. Coptic Chapel of St. Michael. 5. Chapel of St Mary of Egypt. 6. Tomb of Philip d'Aubigny. 7. Main entrance. 8. Forty Martyrs Chapel. 9. Chapel of Mary Magdalen. 10. Greek Chapel of St James. 11. Belfry. 12. Bouillon's Tomb. 13. Post of the Muslim Custodians. 14. Stone of Anointing. 15. Greek Sacristy. 16. Adam's Chapel. 17. Greek Treasury. 18. Chapel of the Mocking. 19. Stairway hewn with Pilgrim's crosses. 20. St. Helena's Chapel. 21. St. Helena Altar. 22. St. Dismas' Altar. 23. Chapel of the Finding of the Cross. 24. Statue of St. Helena. 25. Division of the Raiment chapel. 26. St. Longinus' chapel. 27. Arches of the Virgin. 28. 'Prison of Christ'. 29. Franciscan Sacristy. 30. Chapel of the Apparition. 31. Flagellation Column. 32. Mary Magdalen chapel. 33. Joseph of Arimathea's Tomb. 34. St. Nicodemus Chapel (Jacobite). 35. Three Maries Altar. 36. Armenian Chapel. 37. Rotunda. 38. Holy Sepulchre. 39. Coptic Chapel. 40. Chapel of the Angel. 41. Navel of the World'. 42. Greek Choir (Katholikon). 43. Seat of the Patriarch of Jerusalem. 44. Retro-Choir. 45. Chapel of the Franks. 46. Franciscan Altar. 47. Greek Altar. 48. Altar of *Stabat Mater*.

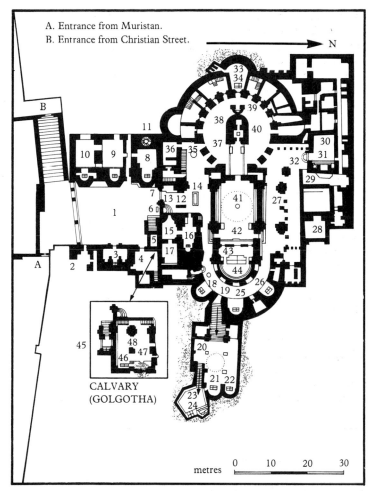

A. Entrance from Muristan.
B. Entrance from Christian Street.

N

CALVARY
(GOLGOTHA)

metres

0    10    20    30

18. The Church of the Holy Sepulchre

*Eleventh Station: Jesus is nailed to the Cross.* At the altar in the right hand nave on Calvary.

*Twelfth Station: Jesus dies on the Cross.* At the Greek altar in the left hand nave on Calvary.

*Thirteenth Station: Jesus is taken down from the Cross.* At the altar of Stabat Mater between the two preceding altars.

*Fourteenth Station: Jesus is laid in the Sepulchre.* Below, at the edicule of the Holy Sepulchre.


## (v) *The Crucifixion and Resurrection: The Church of the Holy Sepulchre.*

Continuing towards the end of the Suq Khan al-Zayt, Zalatimo's Sweet Shop on the right conceals part of the massive fourth century entrance to the Holy Sepulchre. One passes through the outer shop after asking permission: but for a small charge. What remains are tumbled ruins that can only be seen through an ill-lit gap in a recent wall.

Farther on still the street turns right, and then left. Turning right, almost at once one reaches the Russian Mission in Exile, open 9 a.m. until 3 p.m. This contains what is known as the 'Russian Excavations', excavations made in 1883 by the Russian Ecclesiastical Mission in Jerusalem. Passing through a long passage where a small fee is paid for entry, and where there is a bookstall, one reaches what are claimed to be the remains of the Judgement Gate built in the first century BC by Herod the Great, the remains of an arch and two columns, built by Hadrian c.135, part of the Basilica of the Holy Sepulchre as built by the Empress St Helena in 327, and the remains of the house of the Augustinian Canons, who served the Holy Sepulchre before the Franciscans took the work over. The arch is certainly of the time of Hadrian; through it, round to the left and reached by a flight of steps, is part of the platform of his Temple in honour of Venus placed over Mount Calvary in 135. The sill at the foot of the steps, venerated as the gate through which Jesus went out to Calvary, is misattributed, for it cannot be earlier than 135. The wall once had a veneer of marble, described by Eusebius in c.338, and the pitting made by the pins to retain it can still be noted. Constantine re-used the wall as the façade for the atrium of his church, cutting out three doors. The south door is visible, and the columns in the recess opposite belonged to the fourth century portico.

It is perhaps best to visit Zalatimo's shop and the Russian excavations first before continuing down the street past a row of shops and through a narrow door, leading into the present courtyard of the Holy Sepulchre on its south side. It gives one some immediate sense of the violence with which time has treated what Constantine the Great intended to build as the central shrine of Christendom, the place of the Crucifixion and Resurrection of Jesus Christ.

A first century apocryphal work relates that the Empress Protonice, wife of the Emperor Claudius (AD 41-54), a secret Christian, visited Jerusalem, and ordered Calvary and the Holy Sepulchre to be handed over to the Christians. At this stage there was no formal cult round either site. After Titus had besieged Jerusalem in AD 70, the Jerusalem Christians fled with their bishop, Simeon, a cousin of Jesus, but soon returned to the city. The Jewish revolt of 132 led to the total destruction and rebuilding of the city by the Emperor Hadrian. Aelia Capitolina swallowed up the Holy Places: above the Tomb a Temple of Jupiter was built, and one of Venus on Calvary. These authenticated the Holy Places, and were removed only when the plans of the two architects Zenobius and Eustatius began to be put into effect at the orders of Constantine the Great, and under the supervision of his mother Helena. The grand entrance, as has been seen, survives partly in Zalatimo's shop, and led into an atrium in front of a four-aisled basilica. This was built over a cave, now the Chapel of St Helena, with a staircase leading down into the ancient cistern, now the Chapel of the Holy Cross, where St Helena found the True Cross and those of the two thieves. Beyond the basilica again lay a colonnaded garden. On the south side stood the rock of Calvary, surmounted by a Cross. Beyond the garden lay a rotunda surrounding the sacred Tomb. It had three apses and an internal circle of columns. The mortuary chamber was removed, leaving only the slab on which the body of Jesus had been laid. This building was destroyed in 614 by the Persians under Chosroes (Khosrau) II, but shortly restored by the Abbot Modestus. A sixth century representation of the edicule survives in St John Lateran in Rome. It had a conical roof, and above it soared a great dome. Modestus preserved this scheme, as can be seen from a model erected in the Basilica of Aquileia, in North Italy, in the ninth century, where a

93

liturgy special to the city was celebrated at Easter in imitation of that of Jerusalem.

In 1009 the mad Fatimid Caliph al-Hakim destroyed the whole edifice, and it was only in 1048 that a partial restoration was completed by the Emperor Monomachus. The atrium and the basilica were not rebuilt. Calvary remained as a separate chapel in the garden which now became the atrium; while an apse with an altar was constructed on the east side of the rotunda. The Chapels of St. Helena and of the Holy Cross remained, the former being roofed in and lit by a cupola. The reason for the abandonment of so much of the edifice was that the Imperial Treasury could afford no more. As can be seen, this church can only have held a very restricted congregation; thus, the Crusaders undertook a radical reconstruction, and it is this, with but few modifications, that one sees today.

The Crusaders removed Monomachus' eastern apse, replacing it by a splendid triumphal arch. In the former garden this led to a choir, contained within pillars and piers, with an apse at the eastern end, round which was an ambulatory. The Chapel of Calvary was now contained within the new church, and the buildings of Modestus on the north side were also incorporated. About this time the Stone of Unction, where by tradition the body of Jesus was prepared for burial, first appears in literature. In the ambulatory, small chapels recalled different events in the Passion story. Again, on the north side, accommodation was provided for the Augustinian Canons who celebrated in the Latin rite. From the ambulatory a staircase descended to the Chapel of St. Helena and of the Holy Cross; the same staircase that one descends today. Two major restorations were carried out by the Franciscans in 1555 and in 1718. In 1808 a disastrous fire almost wholly gutted the rotunda of the Holy Sepulchre, and, while the Franciscans vainly appealed to the west for funds, the Greeks obtained a *firman* from Ottoman Turkey authorizing them to rebuild it. The present edicule thus replaced the elegant one of former times, and high walls were built to enclose the choir, thus plunging most of the rest of the building into partial darkness. Some ideas of the lightness and airiness of the Crusader building can be obtained – by permission of the Armenians, available from their sacristy immediately on the left of entrance – by going up the stairs into the Armenian section of the gallery round the rotunda. This enables one to look across the top of the

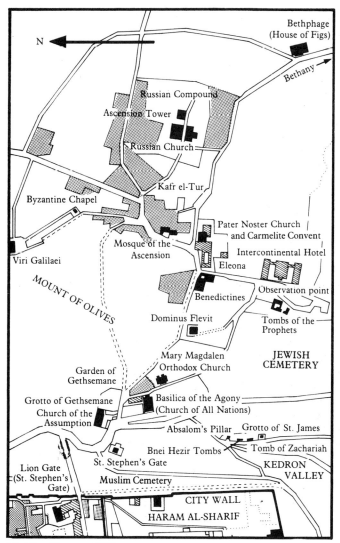

19. The Mount of Olives

enclosing wall, and at the same time to look down upon the edicule of the Sepulchre itself.

The Church of the Holy Sepulchre is opened daily at 4 a.m., and locked at 8 p.m. It is possible to visit it at any time between these hours. Photography is permitted, but flashing lights in the faces of those taking part in the liturgy is understandably regarded as lacking in common courtesy. A sheet showing the times of the celebration of the Orthodox Liturgies and Services here and in other churches is distributed free on request by the Christian Information Centre at the Jaffa Gate. A similar list is provided for Latin Christians of Masses, together with a note of the vernacular in which they are to be celebrated. In the Holy Sepulchre they take place at half hour intervals from 4 a.m. on Sundays in different languages, the Solemn Mass at 5 a.m., as all Solemn Masses here, being celebrated in Latin with readings in Arabic. In addition, many pilgrimages bring priests with them to celebrate for them.

Six communities have the right to celebrate in the Church of the Holy Sepulchre under a *firman* promulgated in 1757 by Ottoman Turkey, and confirmed at the Treaty of Paris in 1855. The intricate regulations determining their rights in different parts of the building are known as the *Status Quo*. There are three major communities, alphabetically in order, Armenians, Greeks and Latins, all sharing certain rights in common, including that to celebrate within the Holy Sepulchre and on Calvary. There are three minor communities, alphabetically in order, Copts, Ethiopians and Syrians. These last only possess the right to celebrate in certain chapels. Under the *Status Quo* regulations they do not give Holy Communion to each other, nor is it permissible for them to do so to members of any other bodies. The Latins are represented exclusively by the Franciscans (Order of Friars Minor). The term Roman Catholic is not used lest it should be misleading, because in Jerusalem there are also Christians of Armenian, Coptic, Greek (Melkite) and Syrian rites in communion with the see of Rome. The three principal communities acted together to repair the church after the earthquake of 1927. In 1934 and 1939 the British Mandatory Government intervened when the building was considered to be in danger of collapse. In 1960 the three communities agreed to repair those parts of the building in their exclusive possession and to contribute to the restoration of those parts shared in common. In this way the rotunda has been almost completely restored, and other parts renovated. Opportunity was taken to make archaeological investigations to throw light on the history of the building. Most notable were the finding of a pagan altar on Golgotha placed there at the Emperor Hadrian's orders, as reported by Eusebius and St Jerome, the exposure of the rock walls of the Chapel of Adam (below, p.98) and the Armenian excavations at levels below the Chapel of St. Helena, which it is wholly impracticable to open to the public because of insufficient space. These show conclusively that the greater part of the church, including Calvary, lies in a disused quarry which was not in use for any purpose in the first century AD, other than for burials. On each of the three sides of the Holy Sepulchre itself are three rock tombs. In one of them two compartments of the type known as *kokim* have been perfectly preserved, and are now known as the tomb of Joseph of Arimathea. The tomb used for Jesus differed from these because it was designed for a single burial only, as stated in the Gospels.

The present entrance to the church is from the south side, through a parvis or courtyard 27 × 18 yards (25 × 17m.). On its south side a mosque built in 1216, with a minaret built in 1417, stands beside the Greek monastery of Gethsemane. The mosque is said to stand where the Caliph Omar prayed in 638. On either side are a number of chapels belonging to the Greeks and Armenians. One enters the courtyard through smallish doorways in the south-west and south-east corners. The Crusader tower is in the north-west corner, and has been truncated, its top having been demolished. In the north-east corner is the so-called Chapel of the Franks, or of the Spasm, the former entrance in Crusader times to Calvary. Immediately in front is a double entrance, of which the right hand side has been blocked. The Crusader tympanum has been removed to the Rockefeller Museum because it was in danger of being totally destroyed by the weather. The right to open and close the remaining door has been the exclusive privilege of two Muslim families since the thirteenth century. They do so in the presence of the Sacristans of the three major communities.

*Calvary, or Golgotha.* Immediately on the right of the doorway a steep stair leads up to Calvary. It has two naves, with stairs in each. The right hand, or southern, nave, known as the Chapel of the Crucifixion, belongs to two periods. The altar area is of the eleventh century, but the part nearer the staircase of the twelfth. This chapel was entirely renovated in 1926, when the marble floor was renewed and the mosaics reconstructed. The altar, of silver on bronze, was given by Ferdinand de Medici, Duke of Tuscany (d.1609). The panels in front are the work of Fr Dominico Portigiani, OP, done in 1588. The candlesticks are of gilded bronze. In the mosaic above the altar a medallion survives of Crusader times, of Christ ascending into heaven. It is here that the Tenth and Eleventh Stations of the Cross are commemorated (above, p.90).

Immediately to the left is the small altar of Our Lady of Sorrows, with a wooden bust given in 1778 by Queen Maria de Braganza of Portugal. The heart is pierced by a sword (Luke 2.35).

Again left is the northern nave, of Calvary. Here the altar of the Greek Orthodox lies across the place where the Cross of Jesus stood, marked with a silver circle round a hole. On either side black marble medallions mark the place of the crosses of the two thieves. Behind the altar is a large icon of the Crucifixion, together with lamps and candles in the Greek manner. Here the Twelfth Station of the Cross is commemorated, and the Thirteenth at the adjoining altar of Our Lady of Sorrows (or *Stabat Mater*) (above, p.90). It is possible to touch the rock where the Cross stood by placing one's hand in the hole. To the right a fissure in the rock is visible, and this fissure can be seen even more plainly below in the Chapel of Adam, which is reached from the staircase on the north side. The fissure is attributed to the earthquake which took place at the moment of Jesus' death (Matt.27.51-2). Either side of the entrance were the tombs of Geoffrey de Bouillon and Baldwin I, King of Jerusalem (1100-18), but these disappeared in the Greek reconstruction of 1810. Near them were the tombs also of Baldwin II (1118-31) and Fulk of Anjou (1131-43); and, beyond, behind the Stone of Unction, those of Baldwin III (1143-62), Amaury I, (1162-73), Baldwin IV (1173-85) and Baldwin V (1173-85). Not a trace of them remains.

*The Stone of Unction.* The position of this stone appears to have been fixed by tradition only in the fourteenth century. In the eleventh century there was a small chapel here in honour of Our Lady.

*The Holy Sepulchre.* Turning left one reaches the rotunda, with the Holy Tomb in the centre. Originally this part of the church was spoken of as the Anastasis, or Resurrection. Between the triumphal arch built by the Crusaders that leads into the Greek choir, and the edicule itself,

**JERUSALEM**, DOME OF THE ROCK
**JERUSALEM**, LA COUPOLE DU DOME DU ROC
**GERUSALEMME**, LA CUPOLA DELLA ROCCIA
**JERUSALEM**, KUPPEL DES FELSENDOMS

166

St. James Printing © Jean — Views of the Biblical World
GARO PHOTOGRAPHIC M.N.

AFFIX
STAMP
HERE

19. Dome of the Ascension, Mt of Olives

18. The Holy Sepulchre

is a raised platform. Two benches flank the front part of the edicule, decorated with monumental candlesticks, and, over the door of the edicule, four rows of lamps. The bottom row belongs to the Armenians, the top to the Latins, and the two middle rows to the Greeks.

The interior of the edicule is divided into two parts. The outer section is known as the Chapel of the Angel. A pilaster in the centre contains a piece of the stone with which the sepulchre of Jesus was closed; the rest has all disappeared in pious hands. Lamps belonging to the three communities hang inside. A very low doorway leads into the tomb chamber itself; on the right is a marble bench, whose top covers the stone on which Jesus was laid. It is this cover, placed there in the sixteenth century, which receives the veneration of the faithful. There are three pictures, each belonging to one of the principal communities, and numerous lamps, among them now some belonging to the Copts. Externally the edicule recalls certain features of its pre-1810 predecessors, of which the earliest example known is a fifth century reliquary which survived at Samagher in Italy.

Behind the edicule is a small Coptic chapel, and, opposite, in the western apse, a Syrian Orthodox altar, and two rock tombs.

*Chapel of the Appearance of Jesus to St Mary Magdalen.* On the northeast side of the rotunda is a chapel of this name belonging to the Franciscans. Originally this event was commemorated in front of the tomb. The commemoration was transferred here only in 1719 (Mark 16.9). Excavations here in 1968 disclosed an Iron Age quarry of c.900-550 BC, and walls belonging to the Emperor Hadrian's buildings of AD 135.

*Chapel of the Appearance of Jesus to his Holy Mother.* Two steps lead up into this chapel which commemorates a pious tradition not found in the Gospels. The magnificent bronze doors, the work of Frank Gatt of Melbourne, were donated by the people of Australia in 1982. The interior was renovated in 1982, when the blue mosaic in the apse was made by two Jewish artists, Mr and Mrs Sabi, of Jerusalem; and a bronze tabernacle erected, the work of Fr Andrea Martini, OFM, of Rome. The chapel dates from the ninth century only. In the south-east corner of the chapel a truncated column is said to be part of the column to which Jesus was tied when he was scourged. The Holy Sacrament is reserved behind the altar. This chapel is used by the Franciscans for singing their office. Each day at 4 p.m. a procession led by the Franciscans visits the principal holy places within the church, and concludes here with Benediction of the Most Holy Sacrament.

*The Latin Sacristy.* Immediately east of this chapel is the sacristy belonging to the Franciscans. In a glass case on the wall the sword and spurs reputed to belong to Geoffrey de Bouillon are kept, for use by the Latin Patriarch in giving the accolade to Knights of the Holy Sepulchre. This may be seen only after application for permission. A priest is on duty either here or in the vicinity at all hours when the church is open. The private quarters of the Franciscans lie behind to the north.

*The northern aisles and the apse.* Behind the Chapel of the Appearance of Jesus to St Mary Magdalen is a gloomy pair of aisles, almost wholly cut off from light by the Greek choir. The right hand aisle belongs to the church of the Crusaders, the left is a relic of the colonnades of Constantine's colonnaded garden. At the far end is a Greek chapel known as the Prison of Christ, for reasons that are obscure. Continuing round the ambulatory are the Greek Chapel of St. Longinus, the Roman soldier who pierced Jesus' side with his spear, and, immediately behind the altar of the Greek choir, the central chapel of the apse, the Armenian Chapel of the Division of the Raiment. To the right a passage leads to a stairway, and immediately to its right the Greek Chapel of the Derision (or Mockery).

*The Greek Choir* occupies the place of Constantine's garden and of the choir built by the Crusaders for the Augustinians. The walls on either side and the iconastasis are wholly modern, built in 1980, in the place of earlier ones. So too are the marble furnishings in the vicinity of the altar, which stands in the chord of the main apse. At the western end a navel-shaped object represents the legendary centre of the earth. This choir is also spoken of as the Greek Cathedral, or *Catholikon*. The throne on the north is for the Patriarch of Antioch, that on the south for the Patriarch of Jerusalem. Some of the marble work was still incomplete in 1986, and there is talk of rebuilding the iconoastasis.

*Chapel of St. Helena.* The stairway mentioned above has twenty-nine very steep steps. In its present form it is a crypt built by the Crusaders in 1130, together with the vaults and the cupola, of which the exterior has already been noted as occupied by the Ethiopians (above, p.90). It is now in the hands of the Armenian Orthodox, and held by them in honour of their national apostle, St Gregory the Illuminator (257-332). It contains two altars and numerous lamps.

*Chapel of the Finding (or Invention) of the Cross.* On the right a narrow, steep, staircase leads down to the chapel in which the Empress St. Helena is believed to have found the Cross of Christ and those of the two thieves. It is quite evidently a former quarry, converted later into a cistern. It is of extreme austerity, particularly as part of the rough quarry walls remain. Behind the plain stone altar a rough-hewn rock pedestal supports a statue of St Helena holding the Cross of Christ, the gift of the Archduke Maximilian of Austria, later Emperor of Mexico (1832-76). This chapel belongs to the Franciscans, who celebrate Solemn Mass there on the two feastdays of the Holy Cross.

## (vi) The Ascension and the Mount of Olives

As one looks across the Kedron Valley to the Mount of Olives, the tall tower of the Augusta Victoria Hospital and another of the Russian Convent dominate the height. Less noticeable, but at the highest point, 2723 ft. (2513 m.) is the Greek Chapel of *Viri Galilaei*, where two columns mark the spot where two men in white garments are said to have addressed the disciples after the Ascension: Ye men of Galilee, why stand ye gazing up into heaven? . . . (Acts 1.11). The tradition first appears in the thirteenth century, and is not solidly established until the sixteenth. To the right of the Russian Convent is the tower of the Church of the Paternoster, and, to its left, the Dome and minaret which mark the former Church of the Ascension. A motorable road winds round at the southern side of the hill, with frequent buses. A steep lane comes up to the top from the Church of All Nations in Gethsemane, and also a rough track already mentioned (above, p.72). Bethany, at the top, seems to have been Jesus' habitual residence when he visited Jerusalem.

According to Eusebius of Caesarea's *Life of Constantine* the Emperor chose three 'mystic caves' to honour the principal Christian mysteries: that of the Nativity at Bethlehem, that of the Resurrection from the Holy Sepulchre, and that 'of the memory of the Ascension upon the top of the mountain.' For early Christians this cave ranked equal to the other two, and here too it was believed that Jesus had foretold the end of the world and had instructed his disciples on many other occasions. The Pilgrim of Bordeaux (AD 333) associated it with where 'the Lord taught his disciples before his Passion', that is, the last discourses in St John's Gospel.

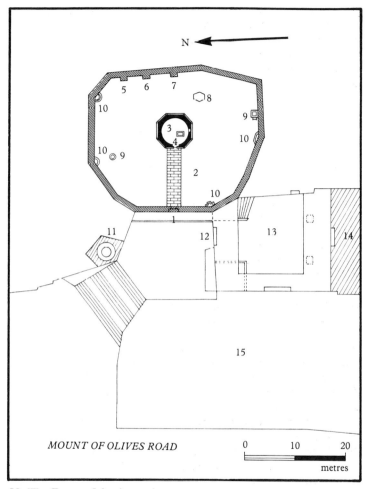

N

5  6  7

8

10

9

3

4

10

10  9

2

10

1

11

12

13

14

15

MOUNT OF OLIVES ROAD

0        10        20

metres

## 20. The Dome of the Ascension

1. Entrance. 2. Paved Path. 3. Dome of the Ascension. 4. 'Footprint of Christ'. 5. Altar of the Armenians. 6. Altar of the Copts. 7. Altar of the Syrians. 8. Altar of the Greeks. 9. Cisterns. 10. Remains of columns. 11. Minaret. 12. Entrance to Mosque. 13. Courtyard. 14. Mosque of the Ascension. 15. Garden.

In 1876 French Carmelite nuns built a convent at the top of the steep lane. In 1910 some excavations revealed the remains of a large basilica 75 yards (69 m.) long and 20 broad (18·5 m.). The nuns had called their church the Paternoster Church, and had inscribed the Lord's Prayer in numerous languages in their cloister. The ruined church behind could be none other than the one the pilgrim Egeria saw in 384, and under it was a crypt cave 'in which our Lord used to teach'; an observation made by many later pilgrims. The last was Sophronius (d. 638), for it was destroyed by the Persians in 614. It was known as the Church of Eleona, a corruption of the Greek *elaion*, meaning of olives. The cave also contains the remains of a first century tomb. The passages leading to it are somewhat confusing, but are very well signposted.

*The Church of the Ascension* lies about 100 yards (c. 100 m.) higher up the hill. The earliest tradition appears to have located the Transfiguration here, and to have associated the Ascension with the *Church of Eleona*. In the fourth century the principal celebrations of the Ascension took place in Bethlehem, but a place called *Inbomon* was venerated as the 'place where our Lord ascended into heaven'. By 392 Poimenia, a member of the Imperial family, had built a circular church here, with its centre open to the sky, surrounded by a monastery. Already by 386 there was a 'shining cross on the Mount of Olives where the Redeemer ascended to his Father'. From the beginning there were footprints here that were venerated as those made by Jesus when he ascended. One now remains in the stone, the other is now to be seen in the Aqsa Mosque (above, p.76). An Armenian account of c.660 tells of a beautiful domed building with three concentric circles, modelled on the Church of the Resurrection. The extent to which this is true is demonstrated by the measurements shown by L. Vincent based on Schick's excavation of 1912, which accord very closely with those of the rotunda of the Holy Sepulchre and, moreover, of the Dome of the Rock as measured by Cresswell. The present building is but a shadow of its former glory, for the Byzantine church had fallen into ruins, and the new building, completed by the Crusaders in 1102, was turned into a mosque by Saladin in 1187. The arcades of the outer octagon have disappeared, and so too have the bases of the pillars found by Schick. Only part of the present surrounding wall follows the foundations of the inner octagon, the rest being of more modern construction, and visibly out of shape. The open arcade of eight pointed arches which originally stood in the centre was walled in by the Arabs. The sacred stone was moved from the centre to one side, and a *mihrab* installed.

On the Feast of the Ascension different Christian communities are permitted to celebrate Mass in the courtyard, while the Latins do so within the octagonal building.

*

Below on the hillside are a mass of cemeteries, chiefly Jewish, and some of great antiquity. The French Benedictines, and, lower down, Russian nuns, have houses here. All these buildings belong to the last or this century. The singing of the Russian nuns is of singular beauty.

## *Other Sites in Jerusalem*

### *The Armenian Quarter*

The Armenian Quarter lies to the south of the square behind the Jaffa Gate, through which one turns right down the Armenian Patriarchate Road. Passing under an archway after the Police Barracks on the site of Herod's Palace, the modern Armenian Seminary and Library, not accessible to visitors, is on the right. On the left a low porch gives access to the walled *Deir al-Arman*, Monastery or Compound of the Armenians, no less than one sixth of the total area of the Old City, which is wholly surrounded by high stone walls. It contains churches, a convent for women, the Patriarchate comprising the Patriarch's residence and offices, residences for clergy and apartments occupied by a number of laity, a printing press and a museum. Except for the latter, most of this is understandably not open to the public, but permission to visit it may be sought in writing from the Patriarchate. It is in fact a city within a city, and the centre for some 2,000 Armenians resident in Jerusalem, as well as being a focus for some six million Armenians throughout the world.

Armenian Christians are believed to have been present in Jerusalem from the fourth century, if not from the third. The nation, then an independent kingdom, was converted to Christianity officially in AD 301. By 634 there were seventy Armenian Churches in Palestine, many of them in Jerusalem. The independent Kingdom of Armenia was partitioned between Rome and Persia in AD 387. The Bible was translated into Armenian in AD 410, and religion as the central focus of Armenian national life was further increased when the Patriarch refused to accept the decrees of the Council of Chalcedon of 451. This was further fortified by the persecution of Armenian Christians by the Persians. Under the Caliphate a number of small dynasties were allowed to arise, one of which survived until it was absorbed by Russia in 1801. Although the Armenians, under their Catholicos, or head, were recognized as a self-governing *millet*, or religious community under the Ottoman Turks, their partition between Ottoman Turkey,

20. Greek Orthodox Church of St John Baptist

21. Garden of Gethsemane

Persia and Russia led, with the rise of nationalism in the nineteenth century, to a desire for complete national unity and autonomy. It cost them innumerable massacres in the nineteenth century, and culminated in the Turkish massacre of two million Armenians in 1920. As a people they have been notable in the arts and architecture; it is to them we owe not only numerous churches, but the walls of Cairo. They have also produced many administrators of outstanding ability, *wazirs* and military and naval commanders.

One enters from the road through a large, dog-legged porch. An Arabic inscription records an edict of the Mamluk Sultan al-Zahir Sayf al-Din Jaqmaq (1438-53) abolishing all taxes paid by Armenians, and ordering his successors not to tax them or oppress them in any way. The second doorway leads into the parvis of the Cathedral of St James. Twenty-two *khatchkars* (excised stone crosses of especial Armenian design) commemorate various events and deaths from 1151 onward. In the porch are two wooden synambres, wooden gongs used before 1840, when the Ottomans had forbidden the use of bells. The cathedral is open to the public only from 3 p.m. to 3.30 p.m. from Monday to Friday, and only from 2.30 p.m. to 3 p.m. on Saturdays and Sundays.

The door opens on a scene of unimaginable splendour. The floor is richly carpeted in purples, greens and reds. The walls are rich with paintings and tiles. The cruciform church is modelled on the tenth century church of Haghpad in Armenia. The rib vaulting of the central cupola appears to be a twelfth century restoration of a building originally constructed in the tenth to eleventh century. The altar, now on the east side, originally lay on the north, the change having taken place when the church passed from the Georgians to the Armenians in the twelfth century. In the north and south walls there are staircases which give access to the upper chapels. On the north side is the shrine of St. James the Great, with richly inlaid doors of tortoise-shell and mother-of-pearl. The shrine itself is of marble, with a stone under the altar marking the place in which his head is buried. On the left is the throne of St. James the Less, used only when the Patriarch is invested and on the feast day of the saint. Ordinarily he uses the second throne beside it. The principal altar is on a raised dais, and it and the whole church is hung with innumerable lamps. The least noticeable but perhaps most elegant features are the small tiles set among the rich Kutahya wall tiling, depicting incidents in sacred Scripture and of lives of the saints. Truly one may say with Jacob: 'How awesome is this place! This is none other than the house of God, and this is the gate of heaven.'

A door on the south side leads into the former narthex, whose arcades were walled up in 1666. It is known as the Chapel of Echmiadzin. Apart from its main altar, a small altar on the right (the altar of Holy Sinai) has three rocks from Mount Tabor, the River Jordan and Mount Sinai, black and greasy with the kissing of many pilgrims, said to have been brought for the consolation of the Virgin Mary because she could not make the pilgrimage to them. Of altogether special beauty are forty-five pictorial tiles of 1719-27 depicting scenes from the Old and New Testaments. This chapel is used chiefly for funerals.

Outside in the courtyard are the Gulbenkian Public Library, with 60,000 books and some 350 periodicals, a Theological Seminary, the Translators' School of St Tarkmanchatz, a library of 4,000 manuscripts and the St James Printing Press (1839), the first printing press in Jerusalem. Farther on through a narrow passage is the Deir al-Zeitun, or Convent of the Olive Tree, known by the Armenians as the Church of the Holy Archangels. It stands on the traditional site of the house of the High Priest Annas. An olive tree in the courtyard is said to be the offspring of a tree to which Our Lord was bound when he was brought here from Gethsemane.

The tradition that it was the House of Annas is not attested before the fourteenth century. The chapel, built (?) c.1300, has an unusually large narthex, and is elegantly decorated in the Armenian manner. In the middle of the north side is a recess with an altar, known as the Prison of Christ. Its tiles, of violet and yellow, are of great elegance. Outside the chapel is a stone that is alleged (and evidently, on the lips of Armenians, with their tongues in their cheeks) to be that which cried out with 'a melodious Hosanna' when Christ answered the Pharisees that the stones would cry out.

Within the Armenian Quarter are several other small chapels. The Yaqubiah Mosque preserves its medieval dedication to St. James of Persia, and lies behind the Anglican Christ Church (1849). Another small mosque was formerly the Armenian church of St. Thomas. Farther away is the Syrian Orthodox Patriarchate Cathedral of St Mark, a small chapel of uncertain date. Elegantly decorated, it claims that a painting on leather of the Virgin and Child is the work of St Luke.

Until it is cleaned it is not possible to date it, but it is possibly Byzantine. Above the church is what is claimed to be the house of Mary, mother of St. Mark, and the Upper Room of the Last Supper. A request to visit it was met with the reply that a priest was asleep there. Our Lady is said to have been baptized in the small baptistery, and St. Peter said to have founded the first church here. This church is open daily from 9 a.m. to 12 noon, but for worship only on Sundays.

Farther down the road from the entrance to the Armenian Quarter is a separate entrance to the Armenian Museum. It is open daily from 10 a.m. to 5 p.m. except on Sundays and holy days. It contains an interesting selection of articles given to the Patriarchate at different periods or brought from different churches, and provides a brief conspectus of Armenian art through the centuries. No other Christian community in Jerusalem displays even a selection of its treasures, and a visit here is something that certainly should not be omitted. A guide remains to be published.

Farther south, outside the city wall, and near the Abbey of the Dormition is the Armenian property of the House of Caiaphas. A new church is being built there on an old site, which at present (1986) is not open to the public. It is of interest only for its associations and funerary inscriptions, of former Armenian Patriarchs and of Patriarchal Secretaries.

## (ii) The Christian Quarter

Unlike the Armenian Quarter, the three remaining quarters, known as the Christian Quarter, the Muslim Quarter, and the Jewish Quarter, are not separated from one another by walls, but simply by the long-standing preferences of habitat.

The principal monuments of the Christian Quarter are the Holy Sepulchre and the buildings nearby, as described in Itinerary VI above. These included the Mosque of Omar (p.97) south of the Holy Sepulchre. On its north side the Khanqah al-Salahiyyah, a dervish convent, was founded by Saladin (Salah al-Din bin Ayyub, whence Salahiyyah) on the site of the Crusader Patriarchal Palace, between 1187 and 1189. Its minaret was erected in 1417, the same year as that of the Mosque of Omar, their tops being identical in structure. Both contain elements of *ablaq* decoration, in which light and dark stone produces a striped effect. In spite of their being at different ground levels, a line joining their tops is absolutely horizontal, and this can hardly be accidental. The mid point of this line falls approximately at the very entrance to the Holy Tomb. One can hardly doubt that this has been contrived deliberately, but the purpose of it is not known. The explanation is probably to be discovered among the more arcane doctrines of Sufi (dervish) mystical theology.

*The Maristan* is so-called because it was a hospice, later hospital, first founded by Charlemagne for pilgrims from the west, and later entrusted to the Knights of St John of the Hospital, or Knights Hospitallers. Thus, originally it was a kind of caravanserai, and the headquarters of the merchants of Amalfi. There were three churches, all built in 1063: St Mary la Latine, for men; St. Mary la Petite, for women; and St. John the Baptist, for the destitute. It was only in 1109 that it became a hospital in the modern sense. The first named of these churches is occupied by the modern Church of the Redeemer, built for the Lutherans in 1898, and incorporating a number of Crusader elements visible in the structure. Saladin lodged in the Maristan in 1187, and made it a *waqf* (religious endowment) for the Mosque of Omar. In 1216 his nephew Shihab al-Din returned it to its use as a hospital, when it acquired its present Arabic name of Persian origin. The adjacent Greek monastery of Gethsemane was formerly the residence of the Grand Master of the Knights. The north side of the Lutheran Church, which, if recent, nevertheless faithfully follows the lines of the earlier construction, incorporates outside a Crusader arch depicting the twelve months of the agricultural year. The Church of St. John the Baptist is entered from Christian Quarter Street. It serves a Greek monastery, and the priest, when available, opens the church. The two bell-towers are a modern addition. The eleventh century structure rests upon the foundations of a church built in the mid-fifth century, and restored after the destruction by the Persians in 614 by John Eleemosynarius. The tradition that it was the house of Zebedee, father of the apostles James and John, is not attested before the fourteenth century. The Roman column at the crossing of the four streets serves as a lamp post, and commemorates Marcus Junius Maximus, Prefect of Judaea, and Legate of the Tenth Legion. It was erected at the beginning of the third century AD by one of his staff, Caius Domitius Sergius Honoratus. The Tenth Legion was stationed for more than 250 years in the Holy City after the capture of Jerusalem in AD 70, in what is now the Armenian Quarter.

## (iii) The Muslim Quarter

The Muslim Quarter comprises 76 acres in the north-eastern part of the city. Much of it has already been described above, for it includes the Via Dolorosa with the Ecce Homo Arch (pp.86-7), the Flagellation Convent (p.88), the Convent of the Sisters of Our Lady of Sion (p.88), together with a large number of Mamluk buildings adjacent to the wall of the Temple area. Often these are marked by Mamluk heraldic emblems; a cup for the Cup-bearer, a napkin set between two horizontal lines in a lozenge shape for the Master of the Robes, and two polo sticks, quite similar to hockey sticks, for the Polo Master. Another set of blazons is to be seen outside St Stephen's gate, known by Christians as the Gate of Our Lady Mary, and by others as the Lion Gate, because of the so-called lions (in actuality panthers, the symbol and nickname of Sultan Baybars (1260-77) depicted either side of it.

The only building connected in any way with the Holy Places so far not discussed is now known as the Church of St Anne. It lies between St Stephen's Gate and the Flagellation Convent, and is used as a Greek (Melkite) Seminary by the White Fathers, who were founded in Algeria by Cardinal Lavigerie in 1868. The modern buildings of the seminary flank the street. Entering the courtyard and passing through it, on the right is the Crusader Church of St Anne, built in 1140. The architecture is that of a French church of this period, beautifully and harmoniously conceived. Unfortunately every decoration has recently been removed from it, and even the plaster from the walls, so that it has a gloomy aspect and a regrettable echo which makes speech in it – other than conversation in close proximity – virtually inaudible.

Below it is a crypt, said to be the home and birth-place of Our Lady. A small cave is shown as her birth-place, and above the altar is a figurine of a babe in swaddling clothes. The tradition, however, appears to have been transferred here from the adjacent ruined buildings and churches of earlier periods.

Leaving the church, and turning right, one reaches an extensive area that has been excavated. St John's Gospel (5.1-13) speaks of Jesus' cure of a man who had been ill for thirty-eight years at the pool of Bethesda, 'a pool with five porches'. Originally there had been a temple here of the god Sarapis (Aesculapius). The White Fathers have erected a painted board which shows the different stages of the buildings disclosed by their excavations. Origen speaks of the five porches c. 231; four round the edges and one across the middle. By the mid fifth century a church in honour of Our Lady had been built there: her home was supposed to be in the vicinity. All this was destroyed by the Caliph al-Hakim in 1009, and the Crusaders found nothing but ruins. First they erected a chapel in the middle of the ruins of the Byzantine church, with stairs down to the northern pool so that pilgrims could venerate it. Only in 1140 did they build the Church of St Anne and the shrine of the home of Our Lady. An inscription over the door records that Saladin turned it into a *madrasa*, or college of higher education for teaching Islam. By the eighteenth century this was in ruins and buried in rubbish. In 1856 the Ottoman Government presented it to France in gratitude for assistance in the Crimean War.

## (iv) The Jewish Quarter

The Jewish Quarter occupies the south-east sector of the city, and is of interest especially for the only visible remains of the terrace on which Herod's temple was built. This is known as the Wailing Wall, or Western Wall. Here the Six Day War, in which the Israeli forces captured the Old City, ended. The area in front, cleared in 1967 (formerly known as the Moroccan quarter), has become the holiest shrine of the Jewish World. It is said that the drops of dew that form on the stones at night are tears the wall sheds while weeping with all Israel.

On the north side of the steps coming from the Wailing Wall was the Church of St Mary of the Germans, founded by German members of the Knights of St John of the Hospital, who in 1190 became an independent order known as the Teutonic Knights, with large territories in northern Europe.

There are several synagogues of ancient foundation. The Ramban and Hurva synagogues are on the ruins of the Crusader Church of St Martin. The Ramban was founded in 1267, when there were only two Jews in the city. The Hurva was founded after 1700. There are four Synagogues built by Sephardi Jews in the seventeenth century, all destroyed and rebuilt since 1948.

The area is worth a visit because of its splendid vistas of the Temple area. Among the ruins one can discern those of the *Nea*, the Emperor Justinian's great church in honour of Our Lady.

## (v) *The Rockefeller Museum*

The Rockefeller Museum (founded 1927), formerly the Palestine Archaeological Museum, is remarkable not only for its collections but also for the intrinsic beauty of its architecture. With an octagonal tower over the main entrance, the galleries are grouped round a cloistered courtyard with a rectangular pool in the centre. It was conceived by the late E.T. Richmond, the first Director of Antiquities under the British Mandate.

There is no comprehensive guide to the contents, but a typed handlist is available on loan at the entrance barrier. The approximate charge for entry is 11 shekels.

The galleries are divided into the following subjects:

1. Entrance Hall: temporary exhibits; exhibit of the month.
2. South Octagon: exhibits from the Late Canaanite Bronze Age.
3. South Gallery: exhibits from the Stone Age, Chalcolithic, and Early, Middle and Late Canaanite (Bronze) Ages.
4. South Room: carved wooden beams and panels from the Aqsa Mosque, 8th century AD.
5. Cabinet of coins of different periods.
6. West Gallery: carved plaster (stucco) and statues from the palace of the Caliph al-Hisham I (788-96) at Khirbet al-Mafjar, near Jericho.
7. Jewellery of different periods.
8. North Room: exhibits from the Israelite Iron Age, and of the Persian, Hellenistic, Roman, Byzantine, Islamic and Crusader periods; reconstructed Middle Canaanite burial-cave from near Jericho.
10. North Octagon: Synagogue inscriptions, 1st to 6th centuries AD; *menorahs* carved in stone, mosaics.
11. Cloisters: various architectural features, sarcophagi, inscriptions on stone, and objects of different periods.

The Museum is open daily except on Mondays and holidays from 9 a.m. until 5 p.m.

# BIBLIOGRAPHICAL NOTE

A full bibliography of Jerusalem and the Holy Land would occupy many volumes. Only a select number of the more important books can be mentioned here. The Bible is indispensable. Kathleen M. Kenyon, *Digging up Jerusalem*, London, 1974, and *The Bible and Recent Archaeology*, London, 1978, are outstanding. D. Bahat, *The Historical Atlas of Jerusalem*, 1976 edn, Carta Ltd, Jerusalem, summarises the history of the city in a series of maps, and summaries of all the sites are given in M. Avi-Yonah and E. Stern, eds., *Encyclopaedia of Archaeological Excavations in the Holy Land*, 4 vols., London 1975-8. Valuable for the history of the land at different times are: J. Bright, *History of Israel*, London, 1967, E.M. Smallwood, *The Jews under Roman Rule: From Pompey to Diocletian*, London, 1976, S. Runciman, *History of the Crusades*, 3 vols., 1951 ff., and a magisterial work by a Christian Arab historian, P.K. Hitti, *History of Syria including Lebanon and Palestine*, London, 1951, from earliest times to that date. Important texts are included in Geza Vermes, *The Dead Sea Scrolls: Qumran in Perspective*, London, 1977. See also Wilkinson's *Jerusalem as Jesus knew it: archaeology as evidence*, Thames and Hudson, 1978, sound archaeologically, but with controversial Christology. G. Le Strange, *Palestine under the Moslems* (1890), reprinted by Khayat, Beirut, 1965, and J. Wilkinson, *Egeria's Travels* (1971), 2nd edn, *Jerusalem*, 1981, and his *Jerusalem Pilgrims before the Crusades*, Warminster, 1977. Concerning pilgrims, of special excellence and charm is H.F.M. Prescott, *Jerusalem Journey: Pilgrimage to the Holy Land in the Fifteenth Century*, London, 1954. A critical and scientific study of the Holy Places and their authenticity is Clemens Kopp, *The Holy Places of the Gospels*, London, 1962 (out of print), and for their ownership the richly documented work of B. Collin, *Receuil de documents concernant Jérusalem et les lieux saints*, Jerusalem, 1982. For these the fundamental work is still L.H. Vincent and F.M. Abel, *Jérusalem, recherches d'archéologie et d'histoire*, Paris, 1914, 1926; and, for particular buildings, a more detailed study, frequently correcting Coüasnon, is V.L. Corbo, *Il Santo Sepolcro di Gerusalemme*, 3 vols., Jerusalem, 1982, with superb illustrations and plans, R.W. Hamilton, *The Structural History of the Aqsa Mosque*, London, 1949, and E.T. Richmond, *The Dome of the Rock in Jerusalem*, Oxford, 1924, and *Sites of the Crucifixion and Resurrection*, 1934. Little attention has been paid to the art treasures of the Jerusalem churches, and B. Narkis, *Armenian Art Treasures of Jerusalem*, Massada Press, Jerusalem, 1979, is of especial interest. The splendid tiles in the Armenian Cathedral have been studied by J. Carswell and C.J.F. Dowsett, *Kutayha Tiles and Pottery from the Armenian Cathedral of St James*, Jerusalem, 2 vols., 1972, with many plates, some in colour. For a detailed guide, Karl

Baedeker, *Palestine and Syria*, last English edition, Leipzig, 1912, is still invaluable for the topography, even if the archaeology is inevitably out of date. In the same way H.V. Morton, *In the Steps of the Master*, London, 1934, remains unequalled for its moving felicity of description. Nahman Avigad, *Discovering Jerusalem*, Blackwell Oxford, 1984, is a most thorough summary of recent archaeological work in the city.

For sites outside Jerusalem, in Bethlehem, Nazareth and Galilee, useful short archaeological guides by Franciscan scholars are available at church bookstalls and at the Franciscan Bookshop close by the entrance to the Latin Patriarchate, Jerusalem. R.W. Hamilton's admirable *The Church of the Nativity at Bethlehem*, 2nd edn 1947, reprinted Jerusalem, 1968, published by the Department of Antiquities and Museums of Israel, is available only at the Rockefeller Museum on special application.

M. Burgoyne, *Mamluk Jerusalem: an architectural study*, with historical research by D. Richards, is a mine of information, especially on the Haram al-Sharif.

22.   Coenaculum, site of Last Supper, Jerusalem

# TABLE OF EVENTS MENTIONED

**800,000 BC to 4,000 BC.** Stone Age

**14,000.** Hunters and gatherers, hitherto nomads, begin to plant grain and domesticate animals.

**14,000.** Galilee Man.

**4,000 to 1,200.** Copper and Bronze Ages.

**c.1,800.** Abraham migrates to Hebron with 318 fighting men.

**c.1,500.** The Hebrews migrate to Egypt.

**c.1,250.** The Hebrews begin to return to Palestine, at the same time as the Philistines arrive.

**1,200 to 586.** Iron Age.

**c.1,020 to 1,000.** The Israelites unite under Saul as king.

**c.1,000 to 961.** David, King of Israel.

**961 to 922.** Solomon, King of Israel.

**c.922.** Schism between the Kingdoms of Israel and Judah.

**c.721.** Israel conquered by Assyria.

**c.688.** Judah abortively attacked by Assyria.

**c.687.** Judah forced into vassalage by Assyria (to c.629).

**605.** Nebuchadrezzar defeats Egyptians at Karkemish.

**604.** Jerusalem pays tribute to Nebuchadrezzar.

**c.597.** Jerusalem surrenders to Babylon: 3,000 deported.

**c.595.** Judaea revolts against Babylon.

**589 to 587.** Nebuchadrezzar besieges Jerusalem.

**587.** Jerusalem sacked. The Temple destroyed. Citizens deported.

**587 to 538.** Babylonian Captivity of the Jews.

**538 to 522.** Cyrus II the Great of Persia allows Jews to return and rebuild the Temple.

**445 to 433.** Nehemiah Governor of Jerusalem: the walls repaired.

**336 to 323.** Alexander the Great, world conqueror: empire extends from R. Danube to India.

**323.** Alexander dies: empire breaks up.

**315 to 200.** Syria and Palestine subject to Egypt.

**200.** Seleucids of Syria take Palestine. High Priests emerge as political figures.

**169.** Seleucids initiate policy of Hellenization in Palestine. The Temple plundered.

**167.** Jerusalem sacked by Antiochus IV.

**165.** Jews revolt under the Maccabees.

**164.** Judas Maccabaeus takes Jerusalem.

**161.** Judas Maccabaeus allies with Rome.

**90.** Maccabaean state collapses.

**63.** Pompey takes Jerusalem for Rome.

**57 to 55.** Jewish revolt against the Romans.

**47.** Herod made Governor of Galilee.

**42.** Herod enlarges fortress of Massada.

**40.** Herod appointed King of Judaea (to 4 BC): Jerusalem greatly enlarged.

**4 (BC) (?).** Birth of Jesus Christ. Herod dies: his kingdom divided between his three sons. Procurators appointed over Judaea (to AD 40).

**AD 26-37.** Pontius Pilate, Procurator of Judaea.

**27 (or 30).** St John Baptist beheaded.

**30 (or 33).** Crucifixion and Resurrection of Jesus Christ.

**40.** Jewish revolt.

**40 to 44.** Herod Agrippa greatly enlarges Jerusalem.

**66.** Jews massacred in Caesarea. Rising in Jerusalem: Roman garrison massacred.

**70.** Following siege, Titus takes Jerusalem. The city sacked and the Temple destroyed.

**73.** Massada falls to Titus: defenders commit suicide.

**132-5.** Jewish revolt.

**135.** Aelia Capitolina built on the ruins of Jerusalem.

**313.** Constantine the Great proclaims Christianity a licit religion.

**327.** Empress Helena 'discovers' the Holy Places. Churches of the Holy Sepulchre and the Nativity begun.

**529.** Samaritans revolt. Church of the Nativity destroyed: rebuilt by Justinian.

**614-29.** Palestine subject to Chosroes II of Persia.

**640-870.** Palestine under the Arabs.

**687-91.** The Dome of the Rock built.

**780.** First stone Mosque of al-Aqsa built.

**870-905.** Palestine under the Tulunids of Egypt.

**905-69.** Palestine again under Arab governors.

**969-1099.** Palestine under the Fatimids of Egypt.

**1009.** Church of the Holy Sepulchre destroyed by Caliph al-Hakim.

**1023.** Church of the Holy Sepulchre partly rebuilt.

**1035.** Mosque of al-Aqsa rebuilt following an earthquake.

**1099.** Crusaders take Jerusalem (to 1187).

**1187-1250.** Palestine under Saladin and the Ayyubids.

**1250-1382.** Palestine under the Bahri Mamluks.

**1291.** Crusaders surrender Acre (Akko), last possession in Palestine.

**1382-1516.** Palestine under the Burji Mamluks.

**1516.** Ottoman Turks take Palestine (-1917).

**1535-8.** Present walls of Jerusalem built.

**1917-48.** Palestine governed by Britain as a Mandated Territory of the League of Nations.

**1948.** 14-15 May, British withdraw: State of Israel proclaimed. War between Israel and Arab powers follows.

**1961-7.** Dame Kathleen Kenyon's excavations.

**1967.** The 'Six-Day War': Israel occupies West Bank of the Jordan. Israel occupies Sinai and Golan Heights.

**1973.** Yom Kippur War: Egyptians reoccupy canal zone in Sinai.

# INDEX

For convenience all the sites in Ain Karim, Bethlehem, Jerusalem and Nazareth are indexed under those places. The Arabic definite article *al*-has been ignored throughout. Letter b. stands for the Arabic *bin*, the son of.

The Beauty of Jerusalem

Galilee, Lake of *see* Tiberias
Gaulonitis 14
Gennesareth, Lake, *see* Tiberias
Georgians 108
Gerizim, Mount 74
Golan 14
Great Rift Valley 42
Greek Catholics (Melkites) 38, 39, 41, 89, 112
Greek Orthodox 26, 28, 45, 56, 57, 84, 87, 88, 89, 94, 96, 97, 98, 101

Hadrian, Emperor 18, 23, 64, 66, 68, 70, 74, 87, 89, 92, 93, 100
Haghpad 108
al-Hakim, Caliph 19, 34, 70, 93, 113
al-Harith (Aretas III) 15
Harvey, W.E. 26
Hasmonaeans 14
Hattin, Horns of 19
Hebrew, Biblical 14
Hebron 11, 22
Helena, Empress St 18, 24, 34, 49, 66, 70, 88, 92
Hermon, Mount 56
Herod Agrippa 68, 87
Herod Antipas 44
Herod Archaelaus 23, 31
Herod the Great 15, 23, 44, 65, 68, 79, 86, 92
Herodian 7, 80
Herodion 22, 30
Hezekiah 12
Hintlian, G 7
Hitler, A. 20
Hoade, Fr E., OFM 84
Houleh, Lake 42
Houphouet-Boigny 79
Huguenot Sisters 41
Hulagu Khan 19

Ibn al-Zubayr, anti-Caliph 74
Idumaea 66
India 14
Indian Ocean 12
Iraq 11
Isaiah, prophet 12
Isam Awadh 7
Israel, Republic of, Israeli 7, 10, 20, 44, 71
Israel, Kingdom of 12
Israelites 11, 44
Israel Museum 44
Issi of Caesarea, Rabbi 49
Italian Government 49

Jacob's Well 45, 57
Jebusites 12, 64
Jenin 56
Jericho 9, 31, 41, 42, 44, 58
Jerome, St 23, 28
Jerusalem *passim*
  Aceldama 82
  Adam, Chapel of 96, 98
  All Nations, Church of 82-86, 102
  Angel, Chapel of the 98
  Antonia fortress 66, 86
  al-Aqsa Mosque 7, 8, 10, 18, 65, 70, 74, 76-78, 104
  Armenian Museum 110
  Armenian 65, 79, 106-110, 112
  Ascension, Church of the 74, 76-78, 102-104
  Assumption, Church of the 84
  Augusta Victoria Hospital 102

  Benevolent Arts Workshop 89
  Bethesda, Pool of 112-3
  British School of Archaeology 7, 64

  Caiaphas, House of 79, 80, 88
  Calvary *see* Golgotha

122